P9-DMS-915

DRUGS, SOCIETY AND PERSONAL CHOICE

Other books by the same authors:

THE AMPHETAMINES

TOXICITY AND ADDICTION

by Oriana Josseau Kalant,
University of Toronto Press, 1966.

EXPERIMENTAL APPROACHES TO THE
STUDY OF DRUG DEPENDENCE

edited by Harold Kalant and Rosemary D. Hawkins,
University of Toronto Press, 1969.

AMPHETAMINES AND RELATED DRUGS:
CLINICAL TOXICITY AND DEPENDENCE

by O.J. Kalant and H. Kalant
Addiction Research Foundation, 1974.

ALCOHOLIC LIVER PATHOLOGY

edited by J.M. Khanna, Y. Israel,
and H. Kalant
Addiction Research Foundation, 1975.

Drugs, Society and Personal Choice

by

HAROLD KALANT

*Department of Pharmacology, University of Toronto
and Addiction Research Foundation of Ontario*

and

ORIANA JOSSEAU KALANT

Addiction Research Foundation of Ontario

with the cooperation of

J. de Lint,
P. J. Giffen,
R. E. Popham, and
W. Schmidt

*of the Research Division,
Addiction Research Foundation of Ontario.*

ADDICTION RESEARCH FOUNDATION

An Agency of the Province of Ontario

Copyright 1971 Harold Kalant and Oriana Josseau Kalant
Reprinted November 1971 and (with corrections) June 1972 and
September 1979.   ISBN 0-7737-7001-1

Reprinted April, 1980.

Published by
Addiction Research Foundation
33 Russell St.
Toronto, Ontario

Printed in Canada

Acknowledgements

The authors wish to record their appreciation to the following authors and publishers for generously granting their permission to reproduce two of the illustrations in this book:

1) To Gerald Klatskin, M.D., and to The Williams & Wilkins Company of Baltimore, for reproduction of Figure 2 from the paper by Dr. Klatskin entitled "Alcohol and Its Relation to Liver Damage", which appeared in Gastroenterology *41*: 445:(1961).

2) To G. Pequignot and F. Cyrylnik and to Pergamon Press of London, for reproduction of Figure 5 from the *"International Encyclopaedia of Pharmacology and Therapeutics"*, Section 20, "Alcohols and Derivatives" (1970). Dr. Pequignot's work was done in association with the Nutrition Section, l'Institut de la Santé et de la Recherche Médicale, in Paris, of which he is chief.

We are also indebted to our colleagues in the Research

Division of the Addiction Research Foundation. We have drawn heavily upon their ideas, and they have provided detailed criticism of the manuscript.

Valuable assistance in locating reference material has been given by Miss J. Hyland of the Research Division of A.R.F.; by the Documentation Section under the direction of Mr. E. Polacsek, and by the Chief Librarian, Mrs. B. Constable.

We are especially grateful to Mr. Leo J. Barry, Miss Joan Hollobon, Mr. John S. Muir, and Mrs. Lucille Silver for their detailed and thoughtful critiques from the point of view of the readers for whom this book is intended.

We are especially grateful to Professor Peter Glassen for his valuable criticisms of the philosophical validity of portions of the book, and to Mr. Leo J. Barry, Miss Joan Hollobon, Mr. John S. Muir, and Mrs. Lucille Silver for their detailed and thoughtful critiques from the point of view of the readers for whom this book is intended.

We also thank Miss M. Brennan, who typed the manuscript; Mr. Alasdair McCrimmon, who prepared the Index; and Mrs. Lois Adair, who edited the manuscript for publication.

Foreword

"Drugs, Society, and Personal Choice" is a book designed to help people—as individuals, as family members, and as policymakers—to arrive at fully informed, balanced, reasonable decisions about drugs. Many scientists today are concerned that their work should contribute to this process. Dr. Harold Kalant and his wife Dr. Oriana Kalant wish to provide through this book data that will assist responsible citizens in achieving a perspective that can lead to an appropriate decision.

The authors carefully refrain from usurping the individual's right and duty to make up his own mind, once he is fully informed. This book is a kind of exercise in achieving perspective; and as such it becomes a significant model for democratic decision making in general, beyond as well as within the field of drug use.

The balance in which all the data must be weighed— laboratory data, social, personal, and ethical data—is the delicate system of *social cost/social benefit* accounting.

Each person must become aware of the full potential of assets and liabilities in every decision before he can exercise his wisest judgment. It is not an easy task, nor one to be taken lightly. And it is not a task that we can comfortably leave to others.

Faced with the need to re-examine and re-define laws dealing with the use of psychoactive drugs, the Government of Canada embarked upon this course of searching out the data and encouraging its discussion by establishing the LeDain Commission on the non-medical use of drugs. The interim and final reports of that Commission are essential components of the process of arriving at new laws for today's society; but these reports take on greater meaning for our legislators when they are accompanied by widespread, well-informed public discussion. The authors of this book, who are distinguished scientists in the fields of pharmacology and physiology and active members of the Addiction Research Foundation staff, have made an important contribution to the clarification of a very vexed and clouded area by preparing this book. It deserves the serious attention of every responsible citizen.

H. David Archibald,
Executive Director,
Addiction Research Foundation,
Toronto.

Preface

The past few years have seen the appearance of a large number of books and articles on marihuana and other drugs. The reason for this flood of publications is not hard to find. Public concern about a phenomenon which has apparently arisen with startling speed and which most people find themselves unable to explain has given rise to intense anxiety and a demand for knowledge and explanation.

Some excellent books have been written. To name a few, Reginald Whitaker's *Drugs and the Law* (5), Erich Goode's *Marijuana* (3), Sidney Cohen's *The Drug Dilemma* (1), and Helen Nowlis' *Drugs on the College Campus* (4) are examples of balanced and reasonable approaches to various aspects of the subject. Others, however, have been written with the specific purpose of winning the reader to a particular point of view. To this end, some of these omit information which might weigh against their arguments. Under the circumstances, it is hardly surprising that a great many people who are not specialists in one or other field connected with the drug question find themselves hopelessly confused. They find one book directly contradicting another and are unable to decide whom to believe.

In July, 1969, the Commission of Inquiry into the Non-Medical Use of Drugs, set up by the Government of Canada and headed by Professor Gerald LeDain, began one of the most comprehensive and intensive official inquiries into the subject of non-medical drug use that has ever been undertaken in Canada or in any other country. In April, 1970, the Commission submitted its Interim Report(2), covering in detail its findings during a review of the published work on the nature of the drugs used and their effects, the extent and patterns of drug use in Canada, and the history of Canadian law with respect to drug use. In addition, they presented preliminary findings from their public hearings across Canada concerning the motives for and causes of drug use. This Interim Report, which is a remarkable document to have been prepared in so short a time, was published with one major purpose—to stimulate a vigorous and well-informed public discussion of the whole subject.

The subject of drug use and the attitudes of society toward it is an intensely complex one in which there are no simple answers. The staff of the Addiction Research Foundation believe that there is need for a thorough public discussion of the basic issues, rather than of the politics and personalities surrounding them. In general, what has been said or written publicly has failed to lay the basis for the formation of a reasoned and comprehensive policy toward drug use; and it is the purpose of this book to suggest ways in which such a basis may be sought.

Two major points will be developed. The first is that the reaction to questions concerning drug use cannot be determined by scientific knowledge alone. Science can discover facts concerning the acute actions of drugs and the consequences of prolonged or heavy use. Scientific investigation can also reveal something about the extent of use, the factors which determine this extent, and the probable consequences of changes in these factors. However, decisions as to whether these effects or consequences are to be considered good or bad and how society should react toward them fall not in the area of scientific fact but rather in the fields of personal and social values, ethics, and political feasibility.

The second point is that every decision or action taken by any society has consequences which go beyond the immediate effect that was intended. No advantage or benefit is ever obtained without some cost. This does not mean merely cost in dollars and cents: it also means cost as measured in terms of the functioning of society and the happiness of its members. Reasonable decision-making on social or political policies should take these costs into account by attempting a balance of the value of what is to be gained and the cost to be incurred. Often the costs lie in the future and cannot be predicted easily. Scientific knowledge can help in estimating these, but in relation to the drug question it must be a very wide range of knowledge obtained from all the branches of medical, behavioral, and social science as well as from history and political experience. With the help of our colleagues in the Addiction Research Foundation we have attempted to draw on all this knowledge in analysing the issues relating to drugs and society.

It is up to every citizen to learn as much as he can about the facts and then to make up his own mind about the value judgments which he will place upon them. If enough citizens go through such a process of learning and evaluation, then society as a whole is in a position to make informed decisions about the policies which it wants its government to adopt.

In a democracy, government can sometimes lead the public in the adoption of new policies, but generally it must follow the wishes of an informed electorate. If government is to be able to discharge its responsibilities with respect to its policies and programs about drug use, then public debate is essential. The purpose of the present book is to put into as sharp a focus as possible for the general public those things which are questions of fact, those which are matters for value judgment, and the ways in which the two interact. It is our hope that the book will encourage the type of discussion which the topic fully deserves.

Harold Kalant, M.D., Ph.D.
Oriana Josseau Kalant, Ph.D.
Addiction Research Foundation,
Toronto, March 1971.

Contents

1
Identifying the Problems

WHAT IS A DRUG PROBLEM?

One of the first things that anyone has to do, if he wants to find his way through the maze of conflict and misinformation about drug use, is to define exactly what he wants to talk about. If we want to talk about "drug problems", we have to make two definitions before we can start. We must define what we mean by a *drug*, and also what we mean by a *problem*.

For many people the word *drug* means simply something which a doctor prescribes for the treatment of disease, or which one can buy for the same purpose in a drugstore without a prescription. By extension from this we also include substances such as heroin and morphine, which were originally and still are used medically for the treatment of pain but which are now also manufactured and sold illegally for use as pleasure-producing agents. People who use the term "drug addict" are most often thinking of users of heroin or of similar substances classed as narcotics by the law.

Yet many of the substances which are most widely used for non-medical reasons, and about which public interest and concern have arisen, have no recognized medical uses and are not sold in drugstores. Moreover, medical scientists generally classify as drugs a great many things which the public has been accustomed to use as parts of the normal diet or as accompaniments of accepted social practices. These include coffee and tea, tobacco, alcohol and various spices. Other chemicals, which for many years were used for domestic or industrial purposes of a totally different nature, have recently been used to induce states of intoxication. These include a variety of industrial solvents, cleaning fluids, nail polish remover, and model airplane glue. It is obvious, therefore, that in delimiting the area to be discussed we must forget old definitions. We shall have to think exclusively in terms of the uses to which all of these substances are now put, rather than the uses which were traditional for them. We shall examine this question in the next chapter.

It is even more important to define exactly what we mean by *a drug problem*. A great many people have remarkably inconsistent ideas about what constitutes a drug problem. For example, there are very few people left in this country who would now maintain that all use of alcohol is a problem. The great majority recognize that most people who use alcohol do so in moderation, without any apparent ill effects from it. The majority would also recognize that some people use alcohol to excess and suffer mental and physical ill effects as a result. Most people would agree that those who drink to excess have *an alcohol problem*. In contrast, a great many people feel that *any* use of such substances as marihuana, LSD, or other drugs which have not been traditional in our society, and for which there is at present no medical use, is a problem.

In a certain sense, they are correct. Problems can be of different types. In connection with the discussion of drug use, it is just as well to recognize that there are in fact two rather different types of drug problem.

First, a *social problem* arises whenever the use of these substances by some members of society puts them in conflict with the rest of society. This may occur either as a result of violation of existing laws or because the use of the drugs involves a clash between the values and moral standards of the drug users and those of the non-users. For example, being arrested for driving while impaired by alcohol or drugs is an instance of conflict with the law. Arrest for possession of marihuana is another instance, but of a somewhat different character in that the legal difficulty arises from mere possession of the drug, rather than from the consequences of using it. Impairment of work by absenteeism due to alcohol, or leaving one's dependents destitute or on welfare, are social problems of a different type. The cost of hospitalization for the victims of medical or psychiatric complications of drug use is yet another kind of social concern, and the illnesses themselves constitute a public health problem.

Second, an individual *medical problem* arises whenever the extent of the drug use is such as to produce injury to the health or mental well-being of the user. This is the sort of problem which is associated with the concept of alcoholism as a disease.

It is very important to differentiate between these two types of problem, because the solutions to them are, by nature, very different. The second type, the medical problem, may ultimately be solved by the careful gathering of sufficient scientific evidence of various types. It is a question of studying in detail the actions of the various substances which are used as drugs. Proper attention must be paid to the acute effects produced by doses of different sizes in a large enough number of subjects to permit statistical evaluation of what a particular dose of the drug is likely to do. Further, it is necessary to observe a large number of subjects over a long enough period of time to learn what consequences, both physical and mental, are likely to occur after *prolonged* use at different levels of drug intake. On the basis of such information it will eventually be possible to give a scientifically valid factual answer to questions concerning the probable consequences of different patterns of use of different drugs. Moreover, out of such research there may very well also come indications as to the best methods of treating the mental or physical problems which may arise.

The social problem, however, cannot be resolved primarily by scientific means. Where the problem is one of conflict between different sets of values, different goals, and different concepts of what society should be, there can be no single absolute answer. The most important response we can make in such a situation is to clarify our thinking by identifying the nature of the conflict and recognizing what component of it depends upon fact and what component is value judgment.

In the social sense it is probably fair to say that a problem exists only when it is identified and called a problem. Most of the present concern about drug use in Canada arose because, rather suddenly, a significantly large number of people began to use illegal drugs (such as marihuana) or legal drugs (such as amphetamines and barbiturates) for non-medical purposes. Since these patterns of drug use are still not an accepted part of the normal social practices of the majority of Canadians, they are seen as a problem.

At the same time, however, the use of alcohol has also increased steadily, even among the youth groups who are commonly pictured as the main actors on the "drug scene"(4). Since alcohol *is* a well-established part of our culture, this increasing use of it does not attract much attention, and it is not seen by many people as a social problem, despite the close similarity between the causes and effects of drug use and alcohol use.

FACT VERSUS VALUE JUDGMENT

From the preliminary remarks above, it should be clear that

anyone who wishes to understand questions of non-medical use of drugs and to form reasonable views about them has to be able to distinguish three different factors that go into the process of decision-making.

SCIENTIFIC FACT

This is the area in which the scientist, the expert clinical observer, the statistician, and anyone else concerned with careful objective observations and measurement make their special contributions. For example, if we determine that a particular dose of marihuana produces a particular change in pulse rate or that a certain percentage of people given a particular dose of alcohol will develop an increase in fat content of the liver, these are matters of fact. They are determined by experimentation or by careful clinical observation. The only place for opinion in such questions is in those borderline areas where one must decide whether a particular effect is present or questionable. This is an area for expert opinion, and the public can do little more than attempt to determine who is in fact an expert and accept the expert's findings.

PROBABILITY JUDGMENT

This is the area in which the expert, with the benefit of his knowledge of a field, makes an "educated guess" as to the probable consequences of a particular action. For example, at the present time there is really not enough knowledge concerning the consequences of long-term heavy use of marihuana to enable anyone to say with certainty what percentage of users are likely to have physical or mental damage. However, the expert scientist and statistician, looking at the available literature, can hazard a reasonable guess about the approximate likelihood of such damage. He can also hazard a reasonable guess as to how a particular type of acute effect of a drug is likely to affect one's health.

A case in point, which is still not completely resolved, is

the question of genetic damage as a result of the action of LSD upon the chromosomes of the user. Those who have no expert knowledge concerning the frequency of chromosomal damage from all sorts of other causes, and concerning the effects of these chromosomal injuries on the genetic characteristics of the off-spring of LSD users, are really in no position to know whether the effect of LSD is to be taken seriously or not. In contrast, the expert in genetics and molecular biology is in a much better position to hazard a reasonable guess as to whether or not the observed effects are likely to carry any significant implications for the well-being of future generations.

Whether such implications are to be considered "good" or "bad", however, involves another type of judgment which lies outside the realm of science—the value judgment.

VALUE JUDGMENTS

These are quite different from fact. They are the result of our whole upbringing, including not only the examples and values of the families and friends with whom we have grown up, but also the religious, political, and philosophical standards to which we have been exposed and by which we are influenced.

Suppose, for example, that it is a matter of fact that a given drug in a certain dose tends to produce a quiet, tranquil state characterized by loss of drive and ambition. Suppose, further, that a scientific probability judgment tells us that it is likely that chronic use of that drug, in the appropriate doses, is likely to make the majority of the users less ambitious, uninterested in acquiring material possessions, and emotionally unresponsive. The question which most of us will be ultimately interested in asking is whether this effect is likely to be good or bad for society as a whole.

The answer is obviously dependent upon what we consider to be "good" or "bad". For example, the traditional view of Europeans and North Americans would be that such an effect is bad because it impairs useful work, diminishes productivity, and lowers the material standard of living of a large number of people who may become charges upon the rest of the society. In contrast, those who find that our present society is overly materialistic, excessively competitive, hard-driven, and devoid of tranquillity and introspection might well find these drug effects desirable.

It is not always easy to separate facts from values. In the example above, both groups may share the basic value that happiness is good, and the wish that most people should be happy. But if they disagree about the facts concerning what sort of behavior makes people happy, then the values they attach to different forms of behavior will also differ.

It is evident from these examples that emotions and personal biases have no role to play in questions of pure fact. If emotion intervenes at all in such matters, it is a hindrance because it may impair the objective gathering of factual evidence. For example, biases and preconceptions may influence the scientists' choice of problems to be investigated and the decisions of award-granting agencies about which investigations they should support financially. Thus, certain important areas may be left unexplored for a long time. In the case of probability judgments, emotions and personal biases are probably impossible to eliminate completely, but ideally they should play as small a role as possible. Obviously, when someone hazards a guess, however well-informed, concerning the probability of a certain event, he is likely to be influenced at least a little by his own hopes or fears with respect to the outcome.

Sometimes, also, scientists combine the functions of probability judgment and value judgment on matters which are so technical that non-scientists are willing to accept their decision. For example, the governments of Canada and the U.S.A. recently banned the use of cyclamates as food sweeteners because of evidence linking cyclamates with bladder cancer. In doing so, they were accepting a combined decision (a) that there was a specific risk of cancer in a certain percentage of users, and (b) that the evil represented by this risk out-weighed the benefit from having available a low-calorie sweetener which could be used in cooked foods for diabetics and for the calorie-conscious. If the public had been asked to decide on the second point, they might possibly have concluded that the benefit from cyclamates meant more to them than the risk. But cyclamates do not stir strong feelings, so that the matter was left to the scientists by default.

In general, the scientist attempts to separate such scientific probability judgments from his own personal attitudes. In contrast, emotions and personal biases are closely related to the third type of question, the ethical or moral value judgment. Emotion is obviously an extremely important factor in many of the decisions we make, and it is quite understandable that this may be the case in areas of value judgment. *The important thing is to recognize where it is appropriate, and where it is not.*

THE SIGNIFICANCE OF QUANTITY

One of the hardest things for non-scientists to consider, when discussing matters such as drug use, is the importance of amounts and numbers. One example is provided by the all-too-frequent arguments about whether marihuana is more or less harmful than alcohol. By its very nature such an argument is useless. Different amounts of alcohol produce different degrees of effect and different degrees of damage. In the same way, different amounts of marihuana produce different degrees of effect, and probably also different degrees of damage. A comparison of the two drugs is therefore meaningless unless one modifies the question by a number of subsidiary questions. How much alcohol compared to how much marihuana? Used how often? By what people? Under what circumstances? Only by asking a series of such questions and carrying out the appropriate investigations in order to answer them can one provide a statement of probability concerning the percentage of users of either drug, at a series of different dose levels, that are likely to run into various types of damage of various degrees of severity. Without this quantitative information the comparison is more likely to be misleading than useful. A case in point is the frequently mentioned comparison between the effects of alcohol and the effects of marihuana on driving ability. This will be considered on page 88.

This quantitative aspect is also extremely important when one comes to the question of social or political decisions concerning the role of government in regulating or controlling the use of mood-modifying drugs. For example, we shall see in a later chapter that the proportion of people using a particular drug who are likely to suffer physical ill effects from its use increases as the total amount of use of that drug increases in the general public. That is to say, when the total use of the drug by a certain population is relatively small, the number of users who suffer ill effects from it is likely to be also very small. But when the total use of the drug by the whole population increases, eventually the proportion of users who suffer ill effects also increases(2). In forming a value judgment concerning the use of a particular drug, therefore, one should know how many people currently use it and how many suffer ill effects from it. But one should also know what the severity and numbers of ill effects would be if the drug use were to increase or decrease markedly through changes in the level of public approval and in legal restrictions. In deciding whether use of a drug is good or bad, and in deciding further *how* good or *how* bad, we are more likely to make a balanced and reasonable decision if we take into account *numbers* and not merely types of effect.

WHO IS AN EXPERT?

One of the most difficult problems the public faces in trying to get valid information and to make decisions about drug use is the welter of conflicting opinions from people who all appear to be experts(1). The problem is complicated by the publicity which the communications media often give to the opinions of well-known personalities in politics, entertainment, sports, or other public activities, even when they have no special claim to being experts on drug matters.

In general, most people would probably agree that an expert is someone with special skill or knowledge in a particular field. Difficulty arises because most of us fail to recognize that an expert's field is usually a rather restricted one. A pharmacologist is expert on the ways in which drugs act on the living organism and on the measurement of these actions. A psychiatrist is expert on the mental and emotional problems which some drug users, as well as many who are not drug users, may experience. A chemist may be expert in synthesizing substances which have powerful drug effects, and in predicting which chemical manipulations are likely to result in an increase or decrease of the drug action. A professor of law may be expert in the history of legislation concerning drug use, and in the problems and injustices involved in the administration of those laws. However, when these and other experts step outside the limits of their own areas of special competence, they are no longer experts. A chemist who synthesizes drugs which affect human behavior and mood is not necessarily particularly competent with respect to problems or inequities in the administration of justice. A psychiatrist who sees only those drug users who are referred to him because of serious emotional problems is not necessarily competent in statistical questions related to the prediction of possible consequences of widespread drug use.

In questions of moral and ethical value judgment it has been traditional to regard clergymen and philosophers as the experts. However, contemporary society is clearly undergoing a rapid change in attitudes toward religion and many other long-established practices and values. Under the circumstances, there do not appear to be any universally accepted experts in such matters. Therefore, every citizen is entitled to form his own value judgments, once he has taken the trouble to learn as many of the facts as he possibly can. Perhaps it would be better to say that *every citizen really has the obligation to form these value judgments for himself*, rather than to leave it to some "expert" to tell him what he should believe.

This statement in itself implies a value judgment by the authors which underlies this whole book, and which we believe most of our readers will share. This is that democracy, imperfect as it may be, is still the most satisfactory form of government for us. If we agree that an enlightened public is a basic requirement for the functioning of a democratic society, then it is obvious that every conscientious citizen has to go through the process of reaching value judgments for himself on many important social questions. Only then can he direct his government, rather than be directed by it.

ROLE OF GOVERNMENT

In recent years governments in many countries have played an increasing role in what they conceive to be the task of protecting individual members of society. In our own country, legislation governing the sale and use of many kinds of drug, and laws creating social welfare schemes such as the Canada Pension Plan and the medicare system, are all examples of government efforts to protect the citizens against illness, accident, and the effects of ignorance or improvidence. The role of government is frequently a controversial one because it raises the issue of individual freedom. Is it true, as some people believe, that the best government is the least government? In an ideal society should each citizen have the maximum possible amount of freedom to do whatever he likes as long as he doesn't harm those about him? Or does the government have an obligation to protect those who are unable to protect themselves against various kinds of misfortune, even if these governmental efforts mean a certain restriction of freedom for other people? This type of argument is difficult to resolve because it is essentially a matter of value judgment.

The difficulty is particularly evident in the case of laws concerning the regulation of non-medical use of drugs. If the harmful effects of drug use were severe, obvious, and widespread, there would probably be no argument about the justification for government intervention. There can be little argument, for example, that it is desirable to control the sale of deadly poisons, such as strychnine. The hazards of unrestricted sale of strychnine are obvious, and it is almost impossible to argue that there would be any benefit resulting from its free availability. In contrast, the widespread voluntary use of substances which alter mood or perception implies that the people who use these drugs derive some pleasure or perceived benefit from them. At the same time the harm resulting from the use of these drugs is not always obvious or particularly widespread; otherwise, most users would be strongly inclined to give them up. Therefore, in deciding whether the use of certain substances should be permitted, or forbidden, or subjected to some type of control, a government should ideally consider all the pleasure or benefit obtained by the drug users as well as all the harm or injury resulting from the drug use(3).

PERSONAL VALUE JUDGMENT

The same process of drawing a balance sheet between positive and negative features of drug use should be the process by which the citizen ultimately makes his own value judgment concerning drug use. The purpose of the present book is to help him to strike such a balance. We shall try to do this by presenting as dispassionately as possible a summary of present knowledge about drug effects and also an indication of how we can estimate the numbers and magnitudes of these effects, what sorts of consequences will possibly or probably result from social reactions to drug use, and how these consequences must be taken into account in evaluating the net effect upon society.

2

Drugs and Their Effects

PSYCHOACTIVE DRUGS

In the first chapter we raised the question "What is a drug?" Because of the wide range of substances which are used non-medically for changing the mood or perception or just for "kicks", it is best to recognize as wide a definition as possible of the term "drug". In the words of the Interim Report of the LeDain Commission(8), "the Commission understands drug to mean any substance that by its chemical nature alters structure or function in the living organism." We have to put certain limits upon that definition because it is obvious that food alters function in a living organism, even though almost no one would consider food to be legitimately included under the term drug. Yet many experts feel that people who overeat to the point of producing serious obesity do so for reasons which are not too different from those which cause others to drink too much, and still others to use marihuana or amphetamines to the point of producing harm to themselves. One might argue, therefore, that food which is taken in amounts beyond those required for the maintenance of normal health is being used as a drug. This is, perhaps, a rather far-fetched definition, yet it illustrates the difficulties in defining exactly what is meant by a drug. It seems to us more useful to say that a drug is *any substance, other than those required for the maintenance of normal health (as opposed to the correction of a disease), which by its chemical nature alters the structure or function of a living organism.*

If we accept this definition there can be little argument that tea and coffee, tobacco, and alcohol are to be classed as drugs. A large amount of scientific literature has established quite clearly that caffeine, contained in coffee and tea, is a stimulant(57) with actions which resemble fairly closely those of amphetamine. Most people use it in such moderation that they suffer no ill effects from its use, but the occasional person drinks so much coffee that he suffers the same symptoms of sleeplessness, nervousness, elevation of blood pressure, and hyper-irritability that can be produced by equivalent doses of amphetamine. The same type of reasoning can be used with respect to the nicotine(71) contained in tobacco, and it is very easy to show that alcohol must also be considered a drug because of its many similarities to the barbiturates and other groups of central nervous system depressants.

The drugs with which we are primarily concerned here are those which are used specifically for their effects on mood, perception, and consciousness. Such drugs are known technically as *psychoactive drugs.* Unfortunately, any classification of this type is in danger of running afoul of human ingenuity, since drugs having very different chemical structures are grouped together only because of the function or the use to which they are put, and such uses can change. For example, dextromethorphan (a drug chemically related to morphine and other opiates) is traditionally classified in pharmacology textbooks as a cough depressant. A dose which is normally sufficient to suppress coughing has almost no detectable influence on pain sensation, mood, or perception, and the drug was therefore not classed pharmacologically or legally with the other members of the opiate narcotic group. However, a few years ago it was discovered by non-medical users that a very large dose of cough syrups containing dextromethorphan could produce mental changes which were sufficiently strong to make continued use of the drug attractive to them. Thus, a drug which would not previously have been classed as a psychoactive agent now became one by virtue of a change in the manner and purpose of its use.

Many other drugs also have effects on the mind if taken in very large doses. For example, digitalis is normally used to increase the force of contraction of the heart in patients with heart failure. In the rather large doses, however, which are sometimes required in severe cases of heart disease, the level of drug in the body may be sufficient to produce a toxic state which includes, among other symptoms, mental confusion and distorted perception(49). But even the most enthusiastic non-medical drug user is unlikely to try digitalis for this purpose, because the other components of the toxic state are so unpleasant or dangerous to life that they would virtually rule out the deliberate use of the drug for the production of its mental effects. We can therefore define *psychoactive drugs* as those which *are used primarily for their effects on mood, perception, and consciousness, regardless of what the normal medical use of such substances may be.*

CATEGORIES OF PSYCHOACTIVE DRUG

At the risk of some over-simplification, we can say that the effects of drugs upon mood generally result from their effects upon the state of alertness and contact with the outside environment. Therefore, mood-altering drugs can be classed into three major groups on the basis of their effects upon this state of alertness and awareness of outside reality.

DEPRESSANTS

These are the drugs which decrease the state of alertness and by this means diminish the impact of the outer environment upon the thoughts and feelings of the user. Such drugs include all those which are normally used as sedatives or sleeping pills, tranquillizers, and agents for the relief of pain. Alcohol, barbiturates, over-the-counter sleeping pills, chlordiazepoxide (Librium), meprobamate (Miltown), narcotics such as heroin and morphine, and a large variety of other drugs are included in these categories.

Although narcotics are included as a subgroup of the depressants, it is important to recognize the difference between the legal definition of a narcotic and the pharmacological and biological definitions. According to the law, a narcotic is any drug which is included in the Narcotic Control Act. *This has nothing to do with the basic type of drug action* because the narcotic legislation includes cocaine, which is a stimulant rather than a depressant. It also includes cannabis (marihuana), which has some depressant action, but of a very different type from that of heroin or morphine. Medically, the term "narcotic" is usually used as synonymous with opium, heroin, morphine, and the other natural and synthetic compounds having the same actions as these substances. In basic biological literature, the same term is used to mean any substance which depresses the overall metabolism of living cells and decreases their responses to environmental stimuli. This last definition would take in all the depressants, including general anesthetics, volatile solvents, pure nitrogen gas, and a large variety of substances which are not normally used as drugs.

For the purposes of this book, we shall stick to the common medical or pharmacological definition and consider as narcotics only the drugs of the opiate group and their synthetic substitutes: such drugs as morphine, heroin, methadone, and meperidine (Demerol).

STIMULANTS

These are substances which increase the state of arousal, so that the brain is exposed to a much larger input of information from the environment, and mental processes are speeded up. Drugs of this type include the amphetamines, coca leaves, cocaine, khat, methylphenidate (Ritalin), caffeine (as found in tea, coffee, and the kola nut) and a few other substances which are rather seldom used.

DISTORTERS OF CONSCIOUSNESS AND PERCEPTION

This category includes several different types of drug which have varying degrees of depressant or stimulant action but which act primarily to alter the *quality* rather than the *intensity* of the user's perception of events occurring within himself and in the environment around him. These drugs are often called *psychedelics.*

One group includes LSD, mescaline, psilocybin, and an increasing number of new synthetic compounds designated by such mysteriously impressive names as DMT, DOM (STP), and TMPP.

A second group includes naturally-occurring materials, such as myristicin and elemicin (which are found in nutmeg and which are converted within the body to chemical compounds resembling some of the LSD group).

A third group includes both naturally-occurring and synthetic materials which are normally used in medicine for their effects on the autonomic nervous system.* The effects

---

* The *autonomic nervous system* is that part of the nervous system which regulates the function of organs that are not normally under conscious control, such as the heart, blood vessels, bronchial muscles, stomach, intestines, and urinary bladder. There are two divisions of the autonomic system: (1) the *sympathetic* division, which has been called the "fight-or-flight" system, preparing the organism for emergencies by speeding up the heart, raising the blood pressure, halting the function of the intestine, diverting blood away from the abdominal organs toward the muscles, dilating the pupils, and so forth; and (2) the *parasympathetic* division, which has mainly the opposite effects, such as slowing the heart, stimulating the digestive functions, constricting the pupils, emptying the bladder, and carrying out the sexual reflexes. Both sympathetic and parasympathetic nerves end mainly on glandular and muscle cells in the various organs concerned, but the muscle cells in these organs are different in appearance from those of the voluntary or skeletal muscles and are known as *smooth* muscle.

of these substances upon the mind were discovered only as consequences of accidental overdose and characteristically include a toxic delirious state, with confusion, disorientation, and gross disorders of thinking. Strong effects upon the autonomic nervous system are present, so that the "trip" is only one aspect of a rather marked physiological disturbance. The drugs in this group include atropine, stramonium and other anti-asthmatic compounds, muscarine, and synthetic compounds such as Ditran (JB-329).

A fourth group consists of the cannabis preparations including marihuana, hashish, and the pure synthetic material tetrahydrocannabinol (THC). This is a more complex group, in that it has some, but not all, of the actions characteristic of all of the other drug categories discussed so far: depressants, stimulants, and distorters.

The actions of drugs that make up these various groups of substances are considered in more detail in the following sections.

ALCOHOL

Ethyl alcohol (ethanol) is probably the most widely used psychoactive drug in the world, with the exception of caffeine. It is formed by the deliberate or accidental fermentation of fruits, grains, potatoes, or other foods rich in sugar or starch. This process has been known and utilized since the dawn of recorded history(42).

According to the methods of fermentation, the nature of the starting material, and the subsequent application of distillation, alcohol is found in a large variety of beverages ranging in strength from weak beers through wines of varying potency to the distilled liquors. A good deal of research has been devoted to the question of whether differing kinds of alcoholic beverages produce different effects in man(17, 55, 65). While there do appear to be very minor differences resulting from the presence of ingredients other than the ethanol itself, almost all authorities are agreed that by far the most important share of the effects of all alcoholic beverages is explainable entirely in terms of alcohol content. On this basis, one 12-ounce bottle of beer, one 4-ounce glass of wine, or 1.5 ounces of whisky or other distilled alcoholic beverage are roughly equal in effect. In the following description, therefore, it does not matter much which type of alcoholic beverage is used, as long as the reader substitutes equivalent amounts with respect to alcohol content.

The actions of alcohol on the nervous system are now generally accepted as being fundamentally the same as those of the general anesthetic agents such as ether and chloroform(30). Alcohol and these other drugs do not act directly upon the cerebral cortex—that portion of the brain which is generally associated with memory, perception, and conscious thought. Rather, alcohol and the anesthetic agents are believed to act primarily upon a system of nerve cells located in the deeper and more primitive part of the brain (brain stem) known as the *reticular formation*.

When appropriate stimuli (such as sound, light, heat, and pain) act on the eyes, the ears, the skin, and other parts of the body, they cause coded information in the form of electrical impulses to pass along special nerve fibres ("sensory pathways") toward the sensory areas in the brain. Branches from these sensory pathways also carry the information to the reticular formation, which functions as an arousal system to alert other parts of the brain to the incoming information. As a result, the incoming sensory information sets off impulses to other parts of the brain in which the new information is matched against memory, so that identification of the stimulus is possible. Other impulses go to areas connected with emotion, so that the incoming stimulus evokes a particular feeling or attitude, and to still other areas which initiate responses by muscles, glands, the heart, and other organs(4, 41) (Figure 1).

Alcohol and other anesthetic drugs depress the function of the reticular formation(30, 36). In the absence of its arousal function, incoming information still reaches the

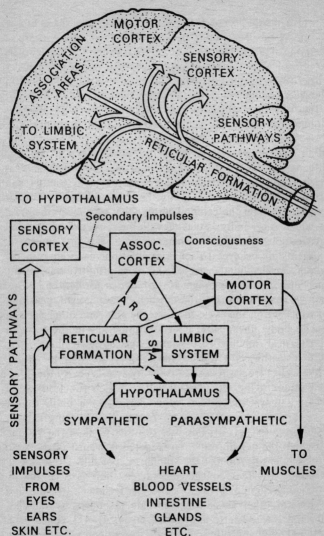

Fig. 1 Schematic illustration of the functional connections between different parts of the brain and nervous system.

primary destination in the sensory areas of the brain, but fails to evoke any of the other responses. When this happens, the person is asleep. If the drug effect is strong enough, the sleep passes into coma or deep anesthesia, or even into death by suppression of breathing. In contrast, if the depression is minimal, then the person is simply less attentive to his environment and more dominated by inner thoughts and emotions than he is in the fully aroused state.

This graded depression of the alerting system is the basis of the varying degrees of intoxication which are seen with different doses of alcohol. It also accounts for the different stages seen during the induction of general anesthesia by ether and similar agents.

In minimal doses, such as an ounce or two of whisky in an adult, the effect is usually one of mild relaxation associated with a decrease in the intensity of alertness toward external environmental stimuli. A number of changes occur which are commonly seen in the onset of normal sleep, such as increased secretion of acid in the stomach, dilatation of small vessels in the skin with a corresponding feeling of warmth and flushing, and minor changes in heart rate. As the person's mental and emotional activities become less controlled by alertness to environmental stimuli, there is a certain freeing or disinhibition of thoughts and feelings. Thus, the user becomes more relaxed and convivial, and conversation becomes animated. This is what is usually meant when alcohol is referred to as a stimulant.

The extent of this effect depends at least partly on the expectations of the drinker. Some people show marked effects with even the slightest whiff of alcohol, and it seems probable that such marked "sensitivity" is really a form of self-suggestion. This is encountered with cannabis and other drugs as well.

With somewhat larger doses, the loss of control over the emotions becomes more marked, but the type of emotion expressed depends upon what the person is feeling at the time; he may become happy, maudlin, aggressive, or amorous, in ways which others may consider rather inappropriate or irrelevant in the situation.

The same depressing action of alcohol on the reticular formation also influences its ability to regulate impulses going from the brain along "motor" nerves to the muscles. Therefore, fine muscular co-ordination becomes increasingly impaired as the concentration of alcohol in the blood and tissues rises. The more complex and rapid the movements, the more easily impaired they are by alcohol.

A similar gradient of effect is seen with respect to mental functions of all types, including the making of rapid decisions. Contrary to a common belief, alcohol does not impair the ability to carry out mental operations such as those involved in mathematical or symbolic reasoning until very high concentrations are reached. If the performance of a complex mental task is being hindered by nervousness or tension, a small dose of alcohol may improve the performance by decreasing the tension. However, it does impair the ability to make the necessary associations *rapidly,* so that if the problems must be solved within a fixed time, the impairing effect of alcohol will be seen even with small doses. For this reason the operation of an automobile or an airplane or other high speed mechanical device is significantly impaired by alcohol concentrations in the blood which are well tolerated in a less demanding situation.

Alcohol illustrates very well the difference between the basic action of a drug and the observed effects upon the mood or behavior of the user. The primary effect of alcohol on the brain is to depress alertness to the environment, reducing the ability to monitor incoming information from different sources simultaneously and to respond rapidly and appropriately. Individuals affected in this manner may behave in many different ways, because people have different preoccupations and emotions just beneath the surface of consciousness and alcohol makes it easier for them to express these different aspects of their mental activity.

The same general principle will be seen in relation to the other types of drugs to be described next. It must be borne in mind, with all of them, that even though the basic action of a particular drug is essentially the same on most people who use it, the manifestations of that action may depend on differences among people and circumstances rather than among drugs.

An interesting example is provided by experimental studies of the effect of slow intravenous injection of dilute alcohol solutions into humans. If several people in the same room receive such injections at the same time, they become talkative, excited, and uninhibited, just as if they had been drinking at a party. If only one person receives the injection in a room by himself, he simply goes to sleep(20, 51).

Another example is the effect of very large doses of amphetamine in mice. This drug is a stimulant (see page 30) which increases the user's level of arousal and heightens the effect of environmental influences on him. Therefore high levels of stimulation from the environment add to the effect of the drug. As we might expect, a dose of amphetamine which a mouse can survive if he is in a cage by himself can be fatal if several mice are placed in the same cage(6).

Alcohol differs from all the other drugs in that, in addition to its action upon the nervous system, it also has an important role as a foodstuff. Alcohol is burned in the liver in the same manner as sugar or pure fat, and accordingly yields energy in the same manner as these foodstuffs(43). Contrary to older views, this energy is available to the body and is readily used. Recent studies at the Hospital for Sick Children in Toronto (73) have shown that severely malnourished infants with congenital or accidental damage to their digestive tracts can be nourished very effectively by the intravenous administration of mixtures containing a high proportion of alcohol. However, alcohol resembles purified sugars or fat in having no vitamins, minerals, protein, or other essential dietary constituents. Therefore, if too large a proportion of the diet is made up of alcohol (as is the case with many chronic heavy drinkers), there is a severe risk of dietary imbalance and of resulting damage to the liver, heart, brain, and nerves as a result of disturbed nutrition(70).

In addition, there is some evidence that alcohol itself

disturbs the normal function of the liver in two ways. The first is that alcohol, in being used as a food by the liver, competes with other food materials for the mechanisms through which they are normally utilized. This competition causes a variety of disturbances in the ability of the liver to handle fat, sugars, and proteins and to synthesize certain body constituents(31, 40). The second mechanism(5, 39) appears to be a direct action of alcohol itself, as a chemical, upon the system by which liver cells secrete fatty materials into the blood stream. This action appears to stimulate the formation of fatty droplets within the cell, some of which reach the cell surface and pass into the blood stream while others accumulate within the cell itself and ultimately damage it.

Wood alcohol (methanol) is particularly poisonous because it is burned in the liver in a manner similar to that of grain alcohol(56). This process converts the methanol to formaldehyde and formic acid, which are extremely damaging to the body, causing permanent blindness in many cases and even death. Most such poisonings occur accidentally, among people who are unaware of the difference between these alcohols.

A great deal of investigation into the actions of ethyl alcohol has been directed toward its effects on the drinker's ability to operate a motor vehicle. This type of investigation has given rise to many studies of the interactions between alcohol and other drugs(54). It is well recognized that many drugs which by themselves produce a similar depression, even if of relatively slight degree, will increase the effects of alcohol when taken together with it. These include not only the barbiturates and other sedatives but anti-histaminic drugs (used for hay fever and other allergies) and tranquillizers of various types. The combination of alcohol with barbiturates or other sleeping pills is responsible for many deaths each year, because of their mutually reinforcing effects on the brain centres that control breathing.

Concern with the effects of alcohol on the driving of

automobiles has also given rise to a great deal of careful study on dose-response relationships—that is, on careful measurement of the degrees of impairment produced at a series of different dose levels(15, 16). For this reason, it is generally understood that one cannot say that alcohol produces a certain effect; rather, one must say *how much* alcohol produces *how much* effect. This is an important point to keep in mind with respect to other drugs, because there has been much less careful work of this nature concerning many of them, especially the "psychedelic" drugs. Consequently many meaningless statements are made with respect to their relative effects.

BARBITURATES AND OTHER SEDATIVES

The first barbiturate sedatives were invented around the beginning of this century, and many hundreds of them, with slightly differing characteristics, have been synthesized in the years since then. Among the most commonly used are phenobarbital, pentobarbital (Nembutal), amobarbital (Amytal), and secobarbital (Seconal). A number of other substances chemically related either to the barbiturates or to alcohol, such as carbromal (Adalin), glutethimide (Doriden), chloral hydrate, paraldehyde, and methylparafynol (Dormison), have also come into widespread use as sedatives or inducers of sleep.

Studies on the functioning of the nervous system suggest that all of these drugs act in a manner similar to that described above for ethyl alcohol(36, 60). Therefore, the characteristic effects produced by these drugs are basically similar to those of alcohol, except for the consequences of the use of alcohol as a food. It is not generally recognized that the sedatives can produce almost exactly the same sequence of behavioral changes as alcohol can, because they are normally used under different circumstances. They are most commonly taken at bedtime, under conditions in which a minimum of stimulation from the environment normally occurs. Therefore, the depression of the arousal system by the action of these drugs leads rapidly to the onset of drowsiness and sleep. If they were taken in the same type of social setting as that in which alcohol is normally used, they would produce the same sequence of changes as are seen with alcohol—those resulting from the gradual reduction in the degree of environmental control over behavior and the increasing freedom of expression of inner-controlled thoughts and emotions. In fact, this type of effect is fairly common among people who use barbiturates and other sedatives regularly during the day.

One important difference among barbiturates and other sedative drugs relates to the rapidity, intensity, and duration of effect of a given dose. Some, such as phenobarbital and barbital, have a slow onset of action and a long duration. This makes them very suitable for prolonged even sedation, or for the control of epilepsy when used alone or in combination with diphenylhydantoin (Dilantin) or other anti-convulsant drugs. At the other end of the spectrum are drugs such as thiopental which have an extremely rapid onset of action, intense effect, and very short duration. Because of this they are given almost exclusively by intravenous injection, as anesthetic agents for short operations or for starting anesthesia which is to be continued with other agents in cases of more prolonged surgery. Between these two extremes are drugs such as pentobarbital and amobarbital which have a fairly rapid onset, intermediate duration, and a sufficiently intense effect that they can be used for modifying the mood in a dose which does not necessarily put the person to sleep if he does not wish to sleep. These differences are very important in determining which barbiturates and sedatives are most likely to be used for non-medical purposes.

TRANQUILLIZERS

The term tranquillizer is applied to a large number of drugs having quite different chemical structures and primary effects, but having in common one important property: relatively a much greater suppressing effect on emotional reactions to stimuli than on general level of alertness(29). In this they differ from the alcohols, barbiturates, and other sedatives. The selective effect upon emotional reactions is probably produced in that portion of the brain known as the limbic system (Figure 1).

It is common to divide this group of drugs into so-called *major* and *minor tranquillizers*. The major tranquillizers include chlorpromazine, reserpine, and the butyrophenones. These drugs appear to have little or no direct inhibitory effect upon the reticular arousal system, and some may even stimulate it slightly. In theory, a drug which has no effect upon the state of alertness but markedly relieves emotional tensions or distress should be a ready candidate for widespread non-medical use. However, most of these drugs are slow in onset or have rather unpleasant side effects on blood pressure and motor co-ordination if given in a large enough dose to relieve tension. For this reason, the major tranquillizers have had little or no appeal for non-medical users seeking an immediate short-lasting change in mood.

In contrast, the minor tranquillizers such as meprobamate, chlordiazepoxide (Librium), and diazepam (Valium) are closer in action to the barbiturates and alcohol; as might be expected, they are often used in a very similar manner. These drugs are among the most widely prescribed in all of medicine(68). The result is that a great many people have come to use them for short-term effects in exactly the same manner as they would use a few drinks of alcohol, and problems of dependence upon the minor tranquillizers have become recognized with increasing frequency in the last few years(13). It is also noteworthy that the complications associated with their long-term use are quite similar to those associated with long-term use of barbiturates or alcohol.

OPIATE NARCOTICS

Drugs in this group have been widely used in clinical medicine for many years because of their ability to relieve distress due to physical pain(27). At the same time, opium and some of its constituents and derivatives have also been used non-medically as mood modifying drugs in many parts of the world. These two kinds of effect are closely related to each other. Scientific study has shown that the effect of these drugs on pain is not primarily a reduction in the sensitivity of the nervous system to pain impulses but rather a reduction in the emotional effect provoked by that pain. Although the subject can feel pain and be aware of it, these drugs enable him to tolerate it with little or no distress. They induce a dreamy, withdrawn, unreal state in which outside influences, such as those which give rise to the pain stimuli, appear to be of little importance or relevance. This same effect is at the root of their non-medical use.

The exact mechanism by which this effect is brought about is not yet known. However, it has been suggested(59) that the narcotic drugs may act directly upon a part of the brain which is referred to by some scientists as the "reward system"(52). If electrodes are inserted into this part of an animal's brain and the animal is allowed to operate a switch which delivers a very weak electrical stimulus through the electrodes into the brain, the animal appears to experience an intense feeling of satisfaction or "reward" which leads it to keep operating the switch incessantly, to the exclusion of activity of any other kind. If morphine does act in a similar way, it might explain why, in experimental animals and to a lesser extent in human beings, the effects of the drug can supplant the satisfaction normally achieved through responses to various biological drives. For example, a hungry animal, when given morphine, is no longer interested in food. In the same way, the satisfaction of thirst, of sexual drives, or of the need to escape from physical injury can all be displaced by the satisfaction produced by the injection of morphine.

Injection is, in fact, the commonest way of giving narcotics. The hypodermic syringe was invented in 1853 for the specific purpose of injecting morphine to relieve the pain of neuritis(24). However, the narcotics can also be taken in various other ways. A solution in dilute alcohol can be taken by mouth, and one such preparation (tincture of laudanum) was very widely used, even without prescription, in England and North America during the nineteenth century(11) and the early part of the twentieth. Opium can be smoked, and this practice was at one time common throughout China and South-East Asia. Even injected, the narcotics can be given either just under the skin (subcutaneous injection) or directly into a vein (intravenous injection), and the results differ accordingly. The fastest onset of drug action is produced by intravenous injection. Subcutaneous injection and smoking cause slower, but still reasonably quick, onset of effect. The slowest onset is noted when the drugs are taken by mouth.

The narcotics also have marked effects upon a number of other tissues besides those of the central nervous system. For example, they tend to depress the function of the smooth muscle (see footnote on page 17) of the gastrointestinal tract, decreasing its ability to propel food and fecal matter along the tract in the normal way. As a result, regular use of these drugs typically gives rise to rather severe chronic constipation. This same property underlies their use in the symptomatic treatment of diarrhea. Many of the drugs in this group interfere with the control of the iris in the eye, and a tightly constricted "pinpoint" pupil is a typical sign of morphine effect. Another physical effect is impairment of the cough reflex and of the mechanisms regulating the depth and rate of breathing. Breathing tends to become shallow, and an overdose ultimately kills the subject by stopping respiration.

Many people receiving morphine for the first time also experience severe nausea or vomiting. This feature often makes the first experiences with the opiates highly unpleasant, unless strongly compensated for either by the relief of pain or by the induction of a much-desired change of mood. It would be quite wrong to imagine that everyone given an injection of a narcotic would find it so irresistibly attractive that addiction was inevitable.

AMPHETAMINE AND RELATED DRUGS

There are two different groups of drugs that are used medically for the relief of emotional depressions. One group is generally referred to as *anti-depressants;* it includes a variety of drugs such as imipramine (Tofranil), amitriptyline (Elavil), and iproniazide. Like the major tranquillizers, these drugs are rather slow in onset of action and usually have to be given for several days or weeks before they achieve their maximum effect(29). In the normal non-depressed individual, most of them have no stimulating action and may even act as mild sedatives. Because of these characteristics they also resemble the major tranquillizers in having virtually no role in non-medical drug use.

The other major group of drugs sometimes used for the relief of depression are the so-called *stimulants,* which act rapidly and affect most people in a similar manner. These drugs include amphetamine and methamphetamine, methylphenidate (Ritalin), and also cocaine, although the latter is not used medically for this purpose because of its toxicity and the risk of causing drug dependence. As we have already noted, it is one of the oddities of the law that even though cocaine acts as a stimulant on the brain and has limited medical use only as a local anesthetic, it is classed as a narcotic by the law. These drugs and a number of others have very similar actions, and therefore a description of the amphetamines alone will probably be sufficient to illustrate the characteristics of all of them.

Amphetamines have an action which is almost directly opposite to that of alcohol and the sedatives: they act on the brain-stem reticular arousal system in such a way as to stimulate its function(3). As a result, the alert, wakeful state is maintained or strengthened, so that the effects of fatigue and boredom are counteracted(75). There is a greater ability to handle the input of information from the environment into the nervous system, and reactions to stimuli are speeded up. Thinking is faster and learning proceeds more rapidly. For these reasons, the person using one of these drugs feels more able to cope with whatever the environment has to offer and, as a result, he frequently experiences a sense of exhilaration and power. This feeling may be highly rewarding to those who would otherwise be fatigued, depressed, or unable to cope with daily problems.

Together with this increased arousal, there are the related effects of diminished need and ability to sleep. Insomnia is therefore a frequent side-effect of these drugs, and many people who use them regularly also take barbiturates at night in order to sleep(32). The amphetamines also inhibit appetite, and for this reason they and a number of closely related drugs are often used to help people stay on reducing diets.

The stimulants resemble adrenaline and noradrenaline, the natural substances which transmit impulses in the sympathetic division of the autonomic nervous system (see footnote on page 17). Accordingly, they produce many effects throughout the body which result from their adrenaline-like action(32). These include dilatation of the pupils, increase in blood pressure and heart rate, relaxation of some types of smooth muscle, and increase in blood sugar. In a certain proportion of users these effects—which give rise to blurring of vision, palpitations of the heart, diarrhea or constipation, together with the restlessness and insomnia already noted—make the overall effects of the drugs highly unpleasant. Such people are therefore unlikely to continue using the drugs for any length of time. In the majority, however, the mental stimulant effects predominate and account for the well-known use of amphetamines by truck drivers on long trips, students cramming for examinations, and athletes attempting to push their performance past the point of fatigue.

Heightened awareness of environmental stimuli, produced by small doses of these drugs, is replaced at higher doses by impaired contact with reality because of the exaggeration of the same drug effects. Thus, overstimulation of the reticular arousal system results in excessive sensory input to the brain beyond the point at which normal mental function can cope with it all. As a result, information pours in faster than it can be assimilated, and the person makes errors of perception due to misinterpretation of this information. Thoughts begin to jump rapidly from one idea to another, and there is loss of continuity in thinking. This state resembles that seen in the psychiatric condition known as manic psychosis. Sensory information is misinterpreted; for example, sensations from the skin may give rise to hallucinations in which worms seem to be crawling beneath the skin, and in this state the subject may severely scratch and injure himself by trying to dig out the imaginary worms. Minor noises may be misinterpreted as voices talking behind the person's back, and out of these he may construct paranoid delusions that people are talking about him or plotting against him. He may even commit violent acts in response to these imaginary events or people. This state, which has sometimes been mistaken for paranoid schizophrenia, can be produced acutely by an intravenous injection of a very large dose of the drugs. Or it may be reached more gradually by chronic oral intake of increasingly large doses over a period of time(9, 12, 32).

Intravenous injection of amphetamines produces an extremely rapid onset of action, accompanied by a sensation of nervous tension throughout the body which is referred to colloquially as a "rush". This sensation, which is usually perceived as highly pleasurable, has given rise to the use of the name "speed" for these drugs(10). This is not a new name but one that was first used many years ago to refer to cocaine, which produces very similar effects.

LSD AND RELATED DRUGS

The drugs of this group are ordinarily taken by mouth.

Within half an hour or so, they begin to produce a rather curious blend of effects which have not yet been adequately explained in terms of their basic actions on the central nervous system(21, 22). All of them have some degree of amphetamine-like effect, which is particularly evident during the first phase after a dose has been taken. This initial phase is usually characterized mainly by physical symptoms such as increased heart rate, dilatation of the pupils, dry mouth, nervousness, and increased reflexes.

This is soon followed by a second phase in which alterations of perception predominate. At first, physical sensations seem to become intensified; colors become sharper and more vibrant, sounds become clearer, and awareness of all bodily feelings is increased. Distortion then sets in, especially in relation to visual stimuli. The reason for this is thought to be partly a direct action on the eye which increases the frequency of impulses coming from the retina, and partly an action on the brain that produces incomplete transmission of these impulses to the cortex. As a result, sizes, shapes, and colors of objects become distorted and appear to be constantly changing. There may be a succession of brilliant colors and sombre dark tones. Objects seem to undulate and to change their relationships to one another in space. The same phenomenon occurs with respect to the sensation of one's own body, so that the hands and feet and head may seem to become enormous in size or to shrink away to almost nothing. With some drugs, such as mescaline, there are brilliant geometric patterns flashing across the field of view(37), which can be seen even with the eyes shut.

The third phase involves disturbance of thought-processes. The distorted perceptions mentioned above may give rise to hallucinations or illusions, such as the feeling that one's body has been left on the ground while the mind is floating away into space. This phenomenon is referred to as *depersonalization*. Orderly thinking becomes slow and difficult, yet the subject often feels that he is having marvellous insights and understanding things he has never understood before. However, attempts to communicate these insights to other people or to write them down for later use usually result in the transmission of muddled, incomplete, or banal thoughts. The vivid visual effects are often experienced as highly rewarding esthetically. The user's mood varies, and he may feel exhilarated, irritable, frightened, confused, or awestruck at different times in the course of the same drug experience.

The effects described above are in varying degrees present in all users and may be considered as closely related to the primary actions of the drug on the nervous system. However, the emotional consequences of these actions may vary widely from one person to another, or in the same person during different drug experiences. For some, the feelings of depersonalization give rise to the impression that the mind is becoming at one with the whole universe. This belief may give rise to a temporary state of ecstasy similar to that which has been described as part of some religious conversion experiences(28). Indeed, mescaline and some of the other drugs in this group are used as a means to just such experiences by certain North American Indian peoples in the rites of the Native American Church(38, 61). Many psychiatrists have explored the use of these drugs in the treatment of psychiatric illnesses(1, 63). They attempt to exploit the temporary changes in the patients' attitude toward other people which may occur during the drug state.

For other people the feeling of loss of close contact with reality is highly disturbing and may provoke either an acute panic state or the onset of a true psychotic reaction(7). The panic state(62), commonly referred to as a "bad trip", is usually of short duration and can be overcome by treatment with chlorpromazine or other tranquillizers and by reassurance or "talking down" by an understanding and sympathetic companion. The main danger is that during the panic the person may injure himself or others by ill-conceived or irrational actions. The psychotic state, however, is probably triggered by the drug rather than caused by it in people with pre-existing mental problems and may outlast the actual drug experience by a very considerable margin.

A further phenomenon, not yet satisfactorily explained, is that of the "flashback". This is most commonly experienced by people who have used LSD or similar drugs repeatedly(35). It consists of a sudden recurrence, in the absence of further drug intake, of perceptual and emotional reactions similar to those which occurred during the drug experience. The flashback was clearly described over a century ago by Ludlow(34), who had taken large amounts of cannabis extract over a period of several years. Another related phenomenon is the ability to recall, almost at will, a less intense version of the same sensations. It may well be that the flashback is a conditioned response to unrecognized environmental stimuli which were unconsciously associated with the perceptual changes during earlier drug experiences.

ATROPINE-LIKE DRUGS

This group of substances produces changes in perception but only as part of a general poisoning resulting from accidental or deliberate overdose(22). As indicated at the beginning of this chapter, all of these drugs interfere with the functioning of the parasympathetic portion of the automatic nervous system (see footnote on page 17). Their major effects are accordingly on organs other than the brain; they tend to produce rapid heart rate, dry mouth and skin, dilatation of the pupils, constipation, inability to empty the bladder, and fever. Along with this general toxic state, large doses produce confusion and delirium, which may include vividly colored hallucinations similar to those which children sometimes experience during a high fever. Thought processes are severely disrupted, and memory is impaired or abolished. The reaction tends to be long-lasting compared to that of LSD and similar drugs, and it is not relieved by a tranquilizer such as chlorpromazine. For most people this combination of events is highly unpleasant. As a result, the drugs are unlikely to be used for their mental effect except by a relatively small group of people who are strongly motivated to use any agent that interferes with normal consciousness.

CANNABIS

A great deal has been written about the effects of *marihuana* and *hashish*(33, 45, 50, 72), and it is probably unnecessary to give a detailed description here. However, a number of points require restatement because of the confusion which has been generated by the highly emotional arguments for and against the use of marihuana in our society(18, 19, 33). It is particularly important in this discussion to bear in mind the significance of dose, as explained in Chapter 1.

Marihuana is normally made by drying the leaves and flowering tops of the hemp plant (*Cannabis sativa*). The dried material is smoked in the form of cigarettes or in a pipe. The major pharmacologically active material contained in the dried plant matter and carried over in the smoke which is inhaled is tetrahydrocannabinol (THC)(46). At a certain stage in the growth of the hemp plant, before the flowers are mature, they are coated with a sticky resinous material that contains a much higher concentration of THC than do the leaves. This resin, gathered from the fresh plant, is dried in the form of cakes of dark brown material known as *hashish*, which has about five to six times the potency of marihuana.

All of these materials can be taken by mouth, but they are not very well absorbed from the stomach and intestine, so that about three times as much material is needed by mouth as by smoking to achieve the same degree of effect(25) and the onset of this effect is considerably slower when the drug is swallowed. Cannabis drugs cannot be injected intravenously in human beings, because they are virtually insoluble in water. This has not stopped a few people from trying (see page 62).

In the small doses in which marihuana or related preparations are normally used, the effects are similar in many ways to those of mild alcohol intoxication. The physical effects are extremely slight and unimportant, either during or after the period of drug effect(58, 74). This fact may make marihuana more attractive than many other drugs. The user feels relaxed and generally less inhibited with respect to behavior and emotional expression. Just as in the case of alcohol, if the drug is used in a social setting it tends to give rise to conviviality, easier conversation, much laughter, and slightly silly behavior. Again, however, as in the case of alcohol, a few people may react with hostility or violence, if these are the emotions they would otherwise control(2). Thus, cannabis probably does not *cause* crimes of violence, but like alcohol, it may permit them to occur if predisposing causes are present within the individual or his environment. As with alcohol, systematic logical thinking tends to be somewhat slowed(58), but cannabis smokers often feel that their minds are actually "soaring" or flitting from thought to thought with great speed. No real impairment of mental abilities is evident at low dosage. A slight suggestion of an amphetamine-like effect is seen in the fact that the heart rate tends to increase, and during this stage the cannabis may intensify the effects of a simultaneously given dose of amphetamine(14).

Many users report that sensations, particularly hearing and vision, tend to be sharpened by the drug, and this is more marked as the dose is increased. With higher doses, five or more times as great as that which normally produces the effects just described, there are perceptual effects which are similar to those produced by the LSD group of drugs described above(23, 26). For example, shapes and colors are reported to be distorted, time and distance seem to be stretched out, and hallucinations of a rather vivid type may appear. Hallucinations, however, tend to be less abstract

and design-like than those produced by LSD and are more
in the nature of reveries or daydreams with recognizable
objects and actions.

When these effects wear off, there tends to be sleepiness
and fatigue, and at this stage of its action marihuana enhan-
ces the effects of barbiturates(69). The whole experience is
usually finished within a few hours, and the subject can
sleep it off and wake up with little ill effect. However, after
large doses, and especially after repeated use, users tend to
feel lethargic and fatigued the next day, and to have little
enthusiasm for normal activities(64, 76). One effect
which has often been described after the cannabis experience is a strong increase in appetite which has not yet been
adequately explained.

Cannabis was used medically during the latter part of the
19th century and the early part of the twentieth(47, 72).
It was given by mouth as a sedative and for the relief of
pain or muscle spasm in a variety of diseases. However, it
gradually fell from favor because the preparations were too
variable and unreliable, so that it was impossible to be
certain of the dose needed to produce the desired effect.
With unusually strong preparations, the normal dose sometimes proved too large, and the medical journals of that
time contain a substantial number of reports of cases in
which the hallucinogenic effects were prominent(72). Just
as in the case of LSD, these effects may be pleasurable or
they may be intensely frightening to people who are not
expecting them and cannot understand why reality suddenly appears to be altered. In the latter case, panic reactions and even the precipitation of a true psychosis can
occur. Similar case reports are beginning to appear in pres-
ent-day medical journals, as non-medical drug users begin to
experiment with more and more potent preparations of
cannabis(48, 53, 66).

Despite the variability in the potency and quality of
different preparations, a small amount of cannabis is still
used medically in several countries(67). Interest in the
medical uses may possibly revive now that pure synthetic

THC is available for careful testing under scientifically controlled conditions.

DOSE, POTENCY, AND MARGIN OF SAFETY

In much of the non-scientific discussion of drug use, there seems to be some confusion about the significance of "weak" and "strong" drugs. LSD is generally used to produce the striking distortions of perception that we have already noted, while marihuana is usually smoked in amounts which cause only mild euphoria. On this basis, many people think of LSD as a strong drug and marihuana as a weak one. However, in scientific terms the strength or *potency* of a drug is expressed in terms of the amount or *dose* required to produce a given degree of effect. *Even a weak drug can produce a strong effect if enough is taken.* Conversely, a powerful drug can produce a mild effect if only a minute dose is used. LSD is indeed more potent than THC, because the dose of the THC needed to produce a hallucinatory state is about 200-300 times as large as in the case of LSD. But there are many known instances of hallucinatory reactions caused by large enough doses of cannabis.

Another important feature which determines the degree of risk attached to the use of large doses of drugs is the *margin of safety.* This is the difference between a dose which produces a desired intensity of mental effect and one which causes toxic or lethal effects. A moderate degree of intoxication usually results from enough alcohol to give a concentration of 100 milligrams per 100 millilitres of blood (0.10 in the Breathalyzer test); death results from a concentration of 500 milligrams per 100 millilitres, so that the margin of safety is roughly a factor of five(30). That of morphine is about the same or a little less(27). With barbiturates, life is seriously endangered by a dose which is fifteen times as large as that normally used to induce sleep(44). Deaths directly caused by minor tranquillizers are rare, and patients have survived as much as thirty times the normal dose of chlordiazepoxide (Librium) or meprobamate (Miltown). In the few fatal cases of amphetamine poisoning that have been described, the dose appears to have been about twenty times the usual medically prescribed dose(32). No human deaths are known to have occurred from overdose of LSD or cannabis, despite the extraordinarily great potency of LSD. Therefore their margin of safety with respect to lethal effects is very high.

These differences help to explain why so many accidental poisonings or suicides are caused by narcotics, alcohol, and barbiturates and virtually none by LSD and similar drugs, even though some of these are among the most potent psychoactive drugs in existence.

3
Reasons Given for Non-Medical Drug Use

ATTITUDES TO DRUG USE

From the description of drug actions given in the preceding chapter, it might appear that the major reason for using any of these drugs is a strong desire to alter one's relationship to the existing environment as it is presently perceived, by increasing or decreasing one's contact with it or by distorting the nature of this contact. This would be a gross oversimplification of the motives for drug use, because many factors are involved besides the pharmacological actions of the drugs.

Some people who are strongly opposed to any use of these agents do in fact regard all such drug use as a form of escapism. They see it, therefore, as socially and psychologically undesirable. This is illustrated by a recent editorial in the *British Medical Journal*(2) which asserted that any drug which modifies consciousness and perception is bad by definition. It is not possible logically to reconcile this view with the acceptance of alcohol, caffeine, and tobacco as part of our normal living habits. We cannot have it both ways. If all use of mood-modifying drugs is escapism, then use of substances such as alcohol must be regarded in the same way. If, on the other hand, alcohol is accepted as part of our normal social environment, then we must be prepared to consider the possibility that the use of other drugs may also be part of a normal, though different, social environment. It will help to keep some balance and perspective in the discussion if we compare reasons for drug use, wherever possible, with reasons for the use of alcohol.

THE SYMBOLIC ROLE OF ALCOHOL AND DRUGS

The use of alcohol has had a long historical development which Jellinek has related to its *symbolic value*(38). The fiery sensation produced by the swallowing of strong alcohol, or the sense of warmth produced even by weaker drinks, are reflected in such names as "spirits" and "eau de vie", and by similar terms that suggest an analogy between alcohol and the spirit of life itself. The symbolic analogy between the red color of wine and the color of blood is seen in the use of wine as a religious sacrament reminiscent of the blood sacrifices of earlier religions. It is not surprising, therefore, that many ceremonies of everyday life dating back to ancient times involve the use of alcohol in one form or another. The drinking of toasts, the use of wine in religious rituals, and the sealing of a bargain with a drink are all easily understandable antecedents of the use of alcohol as a sign of hospitality or friendship.

One reason advanced by some advocates of marihuana use in the USA is that it "cleanses the brain" of the culture and value system of established society and enables the user to see everything anew, without bias. Since there is no scientific support for such a claim, it must be assumed that for these advocates marihuana is really serving a symbolic function in this connection, analogous to that of baptismal immersion in some fundamentalist sects.

ALCOHOL, DRUGS, AND SOCIAL INTERACTION

One of the most widely recognized and accepted uses of alcohol is in the easing of social contacts between people. In a number of cultures other drugs are used for the same purpose. This function of the drugs is at least partly dependent upon their pharmacological actions. Those which are most widely used as social facilitators are generally the milder intoxicants, such as alcohol, marihuana, betel, kola, coca, khat, and opium (in the form in which it can be smoked)(16, 30). These are most commonly used to produce a mild degree of sedation or stimulation; some degree of emotional disinhibition, and a mild euphoria. The feelings of joviality, conviviality, and ease of communication which they produce, when used in low doses, undoubtedly contribute to the widespread popularity of these drugs in social contexts.

In this connection, we have already pointed out that the terms "mild" and "strong", as applied to these drugs, cannot be separated from the question of dose. What we must remember, therefore, is that for normal social purposes, it is the *total dose of drug* which should be small, regardless of whether it is taken in a dilute form (e.g., beer) or in a potent form (e.g., whisky). It is usually easier to keep the dose small if one uses a mild preparation. Probably it is for this reason that dilute preparations such as beer or wine or stronger drinks diluted with water, soda, or other mixers are the ones that are most commonly served. In the same way, marihuana (rather than hashish) and opium (rather than heroin) are the socially used forms of cannabis and the opiates. It is interesting that in China, before the establishment of the present regime, respectable families are said to have been pleased when their sons were moderate users of opium, because it was felt that this would keep them from getting into trouble with gambling and crime.

SOCIAL INFLUENCES FOR CONFORMITY

Closely related to the use of drugs for facilitating social interaction is their use as a *necessary condition for admission* to some social groups. A glass of beer at the pub has traditionally been the "admission ticket" to the society of regular patrons. It provides the feeling of kinship which unites a group of otherwise unrelated or unequal people(36). In the same way, the use of marihuana by many young people in North American society today appears to be related, at least in part, to a desire to show that they belong to the youth culture, as opposed to the orthodox culture of their parents(7, 30). At one point marihuana was a badge of sympathy with, or initiation into, the "hip" culture as opposed to the society of "squares". This latter distinction appears to be less important than formerly, since more and more "squares" are reported to be using marihuana(31).

At the same time, the use of a particular type of alcoholic drink is also a sign of belonging to a particular social group. When we talk of beer drinkers, or the cocktail set, or wine connoisseurs, we are recognizing various drinks as marks of specific social and economic groups. They conjure up corresponding pictures of the clothes their users wear, the language they employ, and the other activities in which they engage.

The desire to belong to a certain group, or to *show* that one belongs to it, is probably an important factor in determining attitudes toward drug use. The example set by one's family and friends is a very strong influence in this connection. Most children in our society grow up with the feeling that drinking and smoking are adult practices and therefore that they have proven their adulthood when they are able to drink and smoke and carry it off. This impression is constantly reinforced by advertising which implies that using a certain beer or cigarette is either elegant, glamorous, or otherwise desirable as a means of enhancing one's prestige. The same type of pressure is constantly provided by one's peer group, from whom one learns the accepted standards of behavior of the group(3, 9). The attitudes of many young people toward the use of marihuana, LSD, and other drugs are similarly determined to a considerable extent by the feeling that it is "with it" to use these substances and a sign of backwardness, by peer group standards, to refuse them(12, 48).

The importance of example in this connection is best illustrated by a recent study carried out by Smart and his colleagues for the Addiction Research Foundation of Ontario(46). In this study, high school students were questioned about their own use of various drugs and about the extent to which their parents used other drugs, including prescription drugs affecting mood or behavior. The students who reported the heaviest non-medical use of drugs by themselves also reported their families as being the most frequent consumers of psychoactive drugs of all kinds, including those obtained by medical prescription. Perhaps this should have come as no surprise, because a similar relation between the behavior of parents and that of their children had already been clearly shown for smoking, drinking, and consumption of various other products(18, 39, 42).

Some caution is necessary in interpreting this finding. It may be, for example, that parents who use large amounts of prescription drugs have emotional problems which they transmit to their children and that these problems also cause the children to use drugs(47). In addition, it must be remembered that parental drug use was as reported by the children and not by the parents. However, this interesting observation suggests that even though the use of marihuana and other drugs by youth is considered in some quarters to be a sign of protest against orthodox society or evidence of a generation gap, it may be that only the *type of drug selected*, rather than the fact of drug use, reflects some element of rebellion. It is also worth noting that alcohol and tobacco continue to be the drugs that are by far the most widely employed by teen-agers, either together with or independently of the use of other drugs(47). One cannot be certain to what extent this is due to easier availability and to what extent it reflects conformity with adult example.

ENHANCEMENT OF PLEASURE

Another reason given by some people for using psychoactive drugs, which may grow out of their initial social use, is the fact that some drugs can increase the pleasure produced by various physical sensations. For example, many people feel that wine adds to the taste of a good meal. In India a drink known as *bhang*, made by grinding cannabis leaves with water, is used by some people for the same reasons(11, 27, 40). Many users report that the heightened intensity of physical sensation produced by marihuana, and by mescaline and LSD during the early stages of their action, leads to an increase in the pleasure obtained from listening to music or from looking at beautiful scenery or works of art(20).

These drugs have also been reported to increase the enjoyment of sexual activity(20). One of the reasons given for the intravenous use of large doses of amphetamine and similar substances is that these drugs permit greatly prolonged sexual activity before the attainment of an orgasm. Probably this effect is the result of the drug's action in delaying the completion of sexual reflexes(28, 32). (See footnote on page 17).

EXPLORATION AND EXPERIMENT

For some people the use of marihuana, hashish and drugs of the LSD type may be part of a general restlessness and a desire for exploration and new experiences. The drug-taking may be only one of many types of adventure or new activity that the user undertakes out of a desire for some change from the routine of everyday life. Sometimes this reason is *given* by people whose use of drugs is really dictated by other motives. However, it can not be denied that in any large group of people there are always a few who seek to explore and test things that are out of the ordinary.

Many famous writers have shown such exploratory interest in drug use. Hashish was first brought to France from North Africa, early in the nineteenth century. A psychiatrist named Moreau de Tours later gave it experimentally to a group of his friends and patients. Among those who used it were a number of famous writers, including Baudelaire and Gautier(26, 33). They regarded the experience as an exciting discovery, and gave detailed accounts of it which were received with great skepticism by their contemporaries(5, 19).

Experiments of this kind are perhaps more characteristic of adolescents than of mature adults, however, and in this sense they are a perfectly natural part of the process of growing up.

ARTISTIC CREATIVITY

Many users of cannabis, LSD, and mescaline claim that these drugs increase artistic creativity(20, 21, 53). Opponents of drug use, on the other hand, draw attention to various experiments in which artistic skills have been judged to be impaired by drug action. The problem is a rather difficult one to resolve, because several different matters are involved.

There seems to be general agreement, even among artists who use the drugs, that the technical skills involved in painting, sculpture, writing, or musical performance may be decreased during the time the drugs are acting. However, the artist's feeling of satisfaction with his own performance or creation may be increased(1, 22, 50). If the work in question is ephemeral, such as a musical performance, the subjective feeling may be the performer's only basis for judging the value of the drug. His liking for it could conceivably mean only that under its influence he was less concerned about the limitations of his own ability.

Creative artists, however, are in a different situation. They may do rough versions of paintings or musical compositions during the drug state and then re-work them after the drug effect has worn off and their technical skills are restored(20). Or they may use the drug experience only as a source of inspiration, transforming this into actual works after the drug effect is over. Since artists may draw inspiration from many different types of experience, it seems reasonable that the novel sensations and perceptions produced by drugs can also feed their creativity. Whether art inspired in this way is better or worse than other art, or simply different, is not our concern here; artistic innovations are usually best judged by posterity.

In any event, there is no reason to believe that any drug can *produce* artistic creative ability where none was present before(5). If it were possible to transform a dull, unimaginative person into an inspired and brilliant artist by such a simple method as having him take a psychedelic drug, the practice would surely have become widespread a long time ago, since peyote and other naturally occurring drugs of this type have been known for centuries.

MYSTICAL EXPERIENCES AND SELF-UNDERSTANDING

In Chapter 2 we noted that the feelings of depersonalization produced by LSD and similar drugs may give rise to a mystical or transcendental experience in which the subject feels an overwhelming sense of unity between himself and all of creation or between himself and God. This feeling became the basis for the use of peyote in ceremonies of the Native American Church(29, 45), as well as of other religions elsewhere in the world. In a less formal way, other sensitive and introspective people may use drug experiences as exploratory activities aimed at understanding their own minds and emotions. Aldous Huxley(23) and others(15) have described vividly such experiences during use of these drugs.

The same type of experience, however, can be obtained by meditation, self-suggestion, prolonged fasting, and other means which do not involve the use of drugs(24). Moreover, it seems probable that the nature of the drug effect is strongly influenced by what the user expects it to be, and his expectations depend in part on the beliefs of the group to which he belongs. Therefore the role of the drugs is not to *produce* such a state but to provide an easier means by which it can be reached. Some former advocates of the use of LSD for this purpose now prefer the use of non-drug methods because in these ways they can achieve the desired state without incurring some of the risks associated with drug use.

It also seems likely that some people give this reason for their use of drugs because it sounds more commendable than a desire for personal pleasure. In other instances the expressed desire for self-understanding may be less representative of a religious or mystical search than of a desire for solution of personal emotional problems.

SELF-MEDICATION

In some cases, psychoactive drugs such as alcohol, barbiturates, tranquillizers, and possibly marihuana are used for reasons that might be regarded as medical in nature, even though not on the prescription of a physician. For example, they are sometimes used to relieve tension or anxiety connected with certain specific and clearly-recognized situations(4, 48). The businessman who has a drink or a tranquillizer to steady his nerves before making an important business deal and the student who takes amphetamine in order to stay awake for prolonged studying before an examination are, in a sense, using these drugs for specific therapeutic reasons. It may not be the therapy which a physician would prescribe, but it is nonetheless aimed at a specific goal.

The Indians of Bolivia and Peru are said to chew coca leaves to ease the pangs of hunger and to increase their ability to work for long hours under severe climatic conditions(52). In a similar manner amphetamines were used by aircrews to enable them to stay awake and alert on long flying missions during World War II(43, 51). The practice was carefully studied and approved by air force physicians, though specific medical orders were not required every time the drug was to be used. In civilian life, however, the use of amphetamines by truck drivers and others for the same purpose is usually a form of self-medication.

However, it seems likely that most use of psychoactive drugs for such quasi-medical purposes is less clearly recognized by the users themselves as a form of treatment. Many people find themselves in chronic states of depression, anxiety, boredom, over-aggressiveness, or other "emotional un-ease" because of unsatisfactory situations at work, at home, or in relation to friends, finances, and other aspects of everyday life. If they are unable to find solutions to these problems, the temporary relief provided by the use of drugs which alter their consciousness or mood may make the continued use of these substances more and more attractive.

Many authorities have emphasized that the heavy user of hashish, LSD, or amphetamines (like the heavy, regular user of alcohol) is likely to be a person with serious emotional or mental problems. A survey of certain marihuana users in Toronto indicated that a very high percentage had recognizable psychiatric illness(34). In the great majority of cases, it seems probable that this illness existed before the onset of drug use and was probably an important factor in determining its pattern.

Specialists are often inclined to react automatically toward such people, classifying their use of drugs as undesirable because it takes the place of proper psychiatric treatment. Before taking such a stand, however, it would seem reasonable to ask what alternatives to this type of self-medication are presently available. There is considerable doubt, today, whether there are enough facilities and trained specialists to provide proper psychiatric treatment for all who require it. Therefore, it may be that drug-taking, at least in some cases, is less harmful to the individual and to society than some of the other things which the same people might do as alternatives.

We have no way of knowing, for example, how many people may be enabling themselves to carry on, in some sort of makeshift way, through the use of drugs who would otherwise "crack up" or commit crimes or suicide, or show some other behavior which we generally consider undesirable. Even if such people did go to their physicians because of emotional problems, it is quite likely that many of them would be given prescriptions for psychoactive drugs. Undoubtedly even symptomatic relief through the use of drugs would be better under medical supervision; there would be less risk of overdoses, psychotic reactions, or physical complications. But we should not dismiss out of hand the possibility that in some cases even unsupervised drug use might be an important safety valve.

SOCIAL UNREST AND DRUG USE

It is commonly stated, and accepted almost without question, that the widespread and increasing use of psychoactive drugs for non-medical purposes is due largely to the stresses and strains of modern life. We constantly read and hear that excessive use of these drugs results from the "rat-race" of competition for better-paid jobs, from chronic anxiety about the possibility of nuclear war, from loss of the firm religious convictions or family ties that helped to stabilize earlier generations, or from "dehumanization" of business, schools, government, or "the system". We are told that young people smoke marihuana or use LSD as a protest against the values of "the establishment", or to assert their individuality in a mechanized society, or even because of the war in Viet Nam.

These explanations may have validity, some more than others, but they are complex reasons which should not be accepted as axiomatic, without careful analysis. Some of them seem to be of too restricted relevance to be very important. For example, the Viet Nam war is of very real concern to American youngsters of military age, but it can hardly be a sufficiently direct influence in the lives of most Canadian, British, French, German or other young people to be a major factor in their drug use. Similarly, the threat of nuclear war has been present for so long that most people appear to have adapted to it, and it constitutes only one of many sources of chronic background uneasiness.

Further, we should ask how or why such factors might be related to individual behavior. Even if all of them generate anxiety, frustration, or resentment, we must still ask why these feelings should lead to drug use rather than to other responses. For example, we might ask why dissatisfaction with a "dehumanized society" or an "unjust economic system" should lead some people to use drugs rather than to engage in vigorous and organized political action designed to remedy these situations. No study to date has in fact shown that these social distresses *are* important causes of drug use by *most* people. Indeed, the Interim Report of the LeDain Commission emphasizes the importance of simple enjoyment as a major reason for the use of alcohol and marihuana(12).

Perhaps the best approach to this problem is to recognize that social stresses of the kind we are discussing are present in the lives of all of us, while the responses we make to them are highly individual and are determined by factors that differ from person to person. As everyone knows from his own experience, the same situation can produce quite different responses in different people.

An extremely interesting example is provided by the very significant differences between men and women with respect to the use of alcohol, tobacco, and drugs. In most societies, women use these substances much less than men do. This is probably not because women have less anxiety, tension or frustration. On the contrary, neurotic illness tends at least to be diagnosed more often in women than in men(13). But Western countries have traditionally disapproved strongly of conspicuous use of alcohol and tobacco by women. In contrast, membership in the club, the pub, and the bar, and the use of strong drinks, cigars, and pipes have been seen as the almost exclusive social prerogatives of men and have come to serve as symbols of masculinity. The net result of these social attitudes has been a much lower rate of alcohol and tobacco consumption by women. Even in countries with a very high rate of alcoholism the great majority of chronic heavy drinkers are men(8, 10, 17). And until recently the incidence of lung and cardiovascular illness attributed to cigarette smoking has been much higher among men than among women(14).

Quite comparable attitudes have prevailed in other cultures where different drugs are used in a social setting. The vast majority of cannabis users in India(11), North Africa(6, 49), and South Africa(41) are men, and the use of khat in Arabia and East Africa seems to be confined almost exclusively to males(25).

The gradual increase in the use of alcohol and tobacco by women in Western countries in the last few decades has paralleled their social and political emancipation. This is well illustrated by the recent television commercial, advertising a special brand of cigarettes for women, which has as its theme: "You've come a long way, baby!"

One kind of drug use by women, however, has traditionally been more accepted than the use of "social drugs". This is the private use of psychoactive agents, either under medical supervision or started by a prescription issued at some time in the past by a physician. Many women today use sleeping pills, stimulants, and tranquillizers much as women in the last century used patent medicines containing opiates. A recent study carried out in Toronto(13) showed clearly that women seek the help of physicians for the treatment of emotional disorders more frequently than men do, and that larger amounts of psychoactive drugs are prescribed for them than for men. In many instances the use of these agents becomes habitual, yet remains socially condoned.

These facts suggest that although the underlying causes of drug use presumably apply more or less equally to men and women in any particular society at any particular time, the decision to use drugs, the choice among them, the amounts used, and the pattern and setting of use are all influenced to a very considerable extent by social factors.

To illustrate this, we can compare the extent of alcohol use in Canada today and during the Depression years in the 1930's. As many will recall, those years were full of anxiety, uncertainty, frustration, anger, and real hardship for a large part of the population. We are told that economic hardship and lack of opportunity are responsible for the growth in drug use in some parts of the population today. Yet the use of alcohol and the frequency of alcoholism during the Depression were much lower than they are now(35, 37, 44). The reason seems to be clear: in terms of the average earning power, alcohol cost relatively much more than it does now, and it was much less readily available. Advertising of beer and spirits was not nearly as extensive, sophisticated, and elaborate, and social attitudes toward alcohol still contained a substantial element of shame or censure. Therefore the anxiety and frustration produced by the Depression must have been expressed in different ways, including riots, marches on Ottawa, and other forms of overt protest. We are not concerned at this point with deciding whether those other ways were better or worse than alcohol or drug use; we shall deal with that question in a later chapter. The point to be made here is that we cannot understand drug use through such simplistic explanations as "social upheaval."

The most reasonable analysis we can make is that the social strains we have mentioned provide a certain level of emotional tension which causes most of us to react in one way or another. But the *form of the reaction* depends on many things, including the influence of example and social approval that we have already discussed.

4

Physical Consequences of Drug Use

ACUTE TOXIC EFFECTS

There is always some risk of confusion in using the words *intoxication* and *toxicity*, because these terms carry certain connotations that are not always clearly recognized even by the people who use them. For example, when we talk about someone being *intoxicated* while under the influence of alcohol, we mean simply that he is showing the character-istic acute effects of the drug. On the other hand, the word *toxic* as applied to most other substances is taken to mean poisonous, and toxic effects are the effects of poisoning. Perhaps the difference in application of these words arises from the fact that most other "toxic" substances are only rarely taken deliberately. However, there is no scientific basis for the distinction. In talking about the psychoactive drugs we shall use the words *intoxication* and *toxic* in exactly the same way as we apply them to the effects of alcohol, to refer to the characteristic psychoactive effects of the drugs. If the effects are relatively mild, then they are

56

simply the usual psychoactive effects ("intoxication" or "high") for which the drugs are taken by the user. However, the same drug effects, if carried to a much more marked degree, give rise to signs and symptoms which we would consider poisoning ("toxicity").

For example, as we pointed out in Chapter 2, the same mechanism of action of alcohol which gives rise to its desired effects is involved in the mechanism by which it can produce death through depression of breathing. The same end result can be produced by barbiturates(23) or other sedatives. We have seen also that this depressant effect is increased by minor tranquillizers, anti-histaminics, and various other drugs when taken together with alcohol or barbiturates. Such combinations account for a great many deaths by accidental or suicidal overdose. Numerous deaths have also resulted from overdose of narcotics. Illicit supplies of heroin regularly go through several middlemen before reaching the user and are usually diluted ("cut") with inactive material by each middleman in turn, in order to increase his profit. Some poisonings are believed to occur when users occasionally obtain undiluted material inadvertently, without being aware of the difference, and take the same amount as they would ordinarily use of the diluted drug.

Exaggeration of the characteristic adrenaline-like effects of amphetamine (increase in pulse rate and blood pressure) occasionally causes death by rupture of a blood vessel in the brain, because of sustained high blood pressure. Other deaths have occurred in athletes because the drug, by postponing the sensation of fatigue, allowed the user to push himself to such extremes of physical exertion that his heart could no longer cope with the load and went into acute failure. Similar incidents have occurred in young children who were accidentally poisoned by amphetamines which they found in exploring the medicine chest(29). This again is an instance in which the same basic action which underlies the effects for which the drug is taken also gives rise to true toxicity when pushed to a higher degree.

In contrast, even though the psychic effects of LSD, mescaline, cannabis, and other drugs with similar actions are dramatic when large amounts are taken, they pose remarkably little acute threat to life. High doses seem to result in very prolonged action but not in sufficient intensification of the physical effects to cause death. For this reason, the few deaths attributed directly to the use of hallucinogenic drugs are mainly accidental deaths resulting from physical injury while under the influence of the drug. For example, the much publicized case of a person who fell to his death from an upper storey window, because under the influence of LSD he was convinced that he could fly, can hardly be viewed as death due to a direct *toxic* effect of the drug. The death was due to a fall, not to poisoning.

An added hazard arises from the constant experimentation which goes on among certain groups. These are primarily young users of hallucinogenic drugs. They often employ a wide variety of chemicals somewhat indiscriminately and in quite unorthodox combinations. In addition, many of the illicit drugs are impure and occasionally contain potentially toxic additions(46). These factors may be responsible for some of the many bad reactions to drugs described in the next chapter, but there is no clear evidence of increased numbers of deaths due to the toxicity of mixed or adulterated drugs.

CHRONIC TOXICITY AND ORGANIC DAMAGE

In a similar manner, one may conclude that in the majority of cases, physical injury related to chronic use of psychoactive drugs is more likely to be indirect than direct.

ALCOHOL

We have already seen in Chapter 2 that alcohol, because it has potentially large but incomplete food value, can replace more valuable items of the diet and result in problems of malnutrition(41). These include peripheral neuritis (a degeneration of nerves in the arms and legs), Wernicke's syndrome (scattered areas of degeneration in the brain, giving rise to defects of memory, thinking, and personality), and degenerative changes of the heart muscle(53, 59). However, recent evidence raises the possibility that some of the liver damage produced by alcohol, particularly that giving rise to cirrhosis of the liver, may be a direct effect of prolonged exposure of the liver cells to alcohol itself(42). This possibility is currently being investigated in a number of research laboratories, and a definite answer cannot yet be given.

CANNABIS

Studies on the effects of chronic heavy use of cannabis are not nearly as complete or thorough as those concerning alcohol, but there is fairly general agreement that the *heavy* user is likely to be physically deteriorated(7). He tends to neglect his personal hygiene and pay little attention to his diet, so that he is likely to become undernourished and therefore more susceptible to infections of various kinds. There is some argument as to whether this physical deterioration is due to the use of cannabis or is a reflection of a state of apathy, dejection, and hopelessness that may contribute to the chronic use of cannabis in the manner discussed in Chapter 3.

Since most observations of chronic heavy users have been carried out in India(7), North Africa(3), and Brazil(11, 54), in areas where a substantial number of people are physically, socially, and psychologically damaged — losers in a fierce competition for survival — it is really difficult to be certain of the correct interpretation. However, experienced observers from those countries generally feel that the chronic use of cannabis does contribute indirectly to the end state in which these people are seen. This impression is strengthened by the results of one experimental study carried out in New York over twenty years ago in which a group of volunteers within a prison were given large doses of marihuana daily for thirty days or longer. During this time they became slovenly and apathetic and began to show neglect of their own physical well-being(63).

So far, there have been no corresponding reports of physical deterioration attributed to heavy use of cannabis in Canada or the United States. This has led many people to conclude that cannabis is a harmless substance, in contrast to alcohol and tobacco(48). However, two things must be borne in mind. The first is that most heavy smokers of cannabis also use other drugs freely, and it is difficult to decide what role each drug may have played in producing any physical complications which they suffer. The second is that cannabis still is a fairly recent addition to the North American drug scene, and that even the heaviest users have been smoking it for only a few years. It is important to remember that some harmful effects of drugs are recognized only after they have been in general use for many years. The thalidomide story is a good example. This drug had been used for some time with patients in general; then, when its use spread to obstetrical patients, the harmful effects of the drug gradually became apparent. Even the barbiturates were used medically for half a century before it was recognized clearly that they could give rise to addiction(16). This point will be considered more fully on page 108.

OPIATES AND AMPHETAMINES

Similar physical changes have been described in the past among chronic users of opiates, either smokers of opium in Asia or addicts injecting themselves with heroin or morphine in the more typical European and North American pattern(6, 39, 44). In these cases, also, the physical deterioration must be considered secondary, because the known effects of the opiates themselves do not account for such changes. Stabilized addicts on regular daily doses of narcotics under medical supervision, provided they pay attention to their diet and personal hygiene, do not appear to suffer any obvious physical injury(52). In contrast, the malnutrition and physical deterioration seen in chronic users of large doses of amphetamine can be directly attributed to one of the characteristic effects of the drug, its property of inhibiting the appetite(12, 37). This property, combined with the mental aberrations that we have described in Chapter 2, provide adequate explanation of the frequent finding of malnutrition in amphetamine users and the consequent signs of infection and other physical disease.

DAMAGE FROM MANNER OF ADMINISTRATION

Chronic physical damage can also result from the manner of administration of a drug, rather than from the pharmacologically active ingredient itself. For example, regular heavy smokers of cannabis, such as those studied in India, were reported to have a greatly increased incidence of chronic lung disease as compared to the rest of the population(7, 30). This is probably attributable to the fact that cannabis smoke is highly irritating and is inhaled deeply and held in the lungs as long as possible to permit the maximum absorption of the active drug.

In general, heavy smokers of cannabis are also inclined to be heavy users of tobacco(45). Therefore it is possible that the increased frequency of lung damage found in these people is at least in part due to excessive use of tobacco(30). However, tobacco is usually selectively bred and processed for its mildness, while no such efforts are made with respect to cannabis. Indeed, the tar content of marihuana smoke was recently found to be 50% higher than that of smoke from tobacco cigarettes of a brand with one of the highest tar levels(16a). It seems quite likely, therefore, that the cannabis itself can make a substantial contribution to the total amount of lung irritation. We can even hazard a reasonable scientific guess that after some years of observation and statistical comparisons it will turn out that the addition of heavy use of cannabis on top of tobacco use will increase the risk of lung and heart disease and of lung cancer in the same way that heavy smoking of tobacco alone does. This is not a wildly alarmist claim, but merely a reasonable guess based on the current views about the causes of these diseases. It is worth remembering, also, that cigarettes were widely used for many years before their relation to lung disease and cancer was recognized.

In an analogous fashion, the use of intravenous injection as a manner of administering such drugs as heroin, other opiates, and "speed" can also give rise to physical injury which is independent of the particular drug used. For example, many users are not especially conscientious about cleaning and sterilizing the needles and syringes which they use. Many also share their equipment with fellow drug users. This sharing of unsterilized needles can spread the virus which causes a severe and sometimes fatal form of hepatitis (liver inflammation).

Other serious illnesses or deaths have occurred as a result of multiple embolism produced by injecting drug solutions containing solid particles that lodge in the finer blood vessels of the brain, lungs, kidneys and other organs. Several cases of this type have recently been reported from the USA(35) and England(25) among young people who were apparently no longer satisfied to use marihuana in the ordinary manner. They prepared a brew of the marihuana in hot water, strained it through coarse cloth which allowed many fine particles to pass, injected this suspension intravenously, and almost immediately became violently ill. They developed sudden fever and chills, jaundice, kidney failure, and severe anemia. Similar episodes were produced by intravenous injection of medicines containing opium and tripelennamine, which were meant to be taken only by mouth for the treatment of diarrhea(62).

DAMAGE TO THE UNBORN

Within the past few years there have been many scientific reports concerning the effects of LSD (56) and cannabis(20, 24, 50, 51) on chromosomes and concerning congenital defects in the children born of drug users. So far, the evidence is not conclusive. There are about as many reports that LSD *does* cause chromosomal damage as there are that it *does not.* There have been a few case reports of infants born with birth defects to mothers who had used LSD or hashish during critical stages of pregnancy(20, 24). However, there is no proof that these defects were due to the use of the drug or, if they were, that the defects resulted from chromosomal damage. This question is important, because some types of congenital damage to newborn children are produced by direct effects of drugs upon the unborn child itself, during the pregnancy, rather than upon the egg cells of the mother or the sperm cells of the father before conception. The thalidomide story is an illustration of this. In such cases, even if the drug is responsible, the same parents can later have perfectly normal children as long as the drug is not used. However, if the defect results from chromosomal damage to the parents' reproductive cells, and if this damage is not reversible after the drug is removed, then all children born of those parents may have a high risk of abnormality. This question is still not satisfactorily answered in the case of psychoactive drugs, so that it would be inaccurate to leave the impression that they have been proven either hazardous or safe in this respect.

TOLERANCE AND PHYSICAL DEPENDENCE

The chronic use of some drugs leads to a change in the user that renders him less sensitive to their effects, so that he has to increase the dose in order to achieve the same degree of effect that he initially produced with a small dose. This reduction in sensitivity to the drug is known as *acquired tolerance.* It can be due to at least two different mechanisms, metabolic tolerance and CNS (central nervous system) tolerance, which are quite different in significance.

METABOLIC TOLERANCE

This consists of an increase in the activity of the mechanisms in the liver and other tissues by which the drugs are metabolically destroyed. In the case of some drugs, including certain barbiturates and to a lesser extent alcohol, this type of tolerance can be a fairly rapid and quantitatively rather important process(10, 34). From the point of view of the user, however, it is simply equivalent to taking a smaller dose of the drug, because if more of it is metabolically destroyed in a given time, then less of it remains in the body to exert its characteristic action.

CNS TOLERANCE

The other major mechanism of tolerance, which is much more important from the point of view of the drug user's well-being, is an adaptive change in the central nervous system which compensates for the effects of the drug and thus renders the user less sensitive to it. For example, chronic use of many drugs of the depressant group, including the narcotics, alcohol, barbiturates, other sedatives, and the minor tranquillizers, leads to a compensatory increase in the excitability of nerve cells, offsetting the decrease in excitability produced by the drugs. The user must then take a larger dose in order to achieve the depressant effect he seeks.

When the drug is removed the increased excitability of the nerve cells remains for some time afterward. But now, instead of being a beneficial compensation for the effects of the drug, it is actually a disturbing phenomenon in its own right because it leaves the undrugged nerve cells excessively responsive to normal stimuli. As a result, the person becomes hyperexcitable, jittery, unable to sleep, and bothered by various signs of overactivity of the autonomic nervous system (see page 17), including sweating, nausea, and palpitations of the heart. In the case of opiate withdrawal, one such autonomic effect causes the smooth muscle of the hair follicles to contract, making the hair on the body bristle and accounting for the well-known term "cold turkey" which is applied to the withdrawal reaction in opiate addicts(20). In the case of barbiturates and alcohol, the more severe signs of nervous system overactivity include tremor, convulsions, and hallucinations, all of which are seen in fully developed cases of delirium tremens, which is sometimes fatal(60). Similar symptoms have been reported as withdrawal reactions from minor tranquillizers and from non-barbiturate sedatives(15).

Most chronic drug users learn to recognize the early symptoms of such withdrawal reactions. They learn that by taking more drug they can cause these symptoms to disappear, because they are again balancing off the over-reactivity of the nervous system against the actions of the drugs. In this case, they are using the drugs as a form of treatment for the changes that were responsible for drug tolerance. In this state they are said to be *physically dependent* upon the drugs, in the sense that if they do not take them they will suffer the corresponding withdrawal reactions.

Tolerance to amphetamines can reach remarkable levels(29, 38). For example, the normal medically pre-scribed dose of amphetamine is 5 to 10 milligrams.* With chronic use, whether by mouth or by intravenous injection, the tolerance can build up to a level such that the user can tolerate hundreds of milligrams* with relatively mild phys-ical effects. Undoubtedly, some speed users tell grossly exaggerated stories, partly to gain prestige in a drug-using group and partly through ignorance. Some have reported using over a gram at a time by intravenous injection, and there is even one claim of 15 grams, or 1,500 to 3,000 times the normally prescribed dose(38). However, a number of samples sold by illicit drug dealers as a "gram" of methamphetamine were recently analyzed in the Addiction Research Foundation(21). It was found that the average weight of the so-called gram was only 200 milligrams, or one-fifth of a gram. Thus, it appears that the doses used intravenously by speed addicts are not very different from those used by addicts who take the drug by mouth. The main difference appears to be in the immediate conse-quences of the "rush" which was mentioned in Chapter 2 and will be discussed more fully in the next chapter.

* Note: 1 gram = 1000 milligrams; an ounce = 28 grams; one grain = 60 milligrams.

The nature of the tolerance to amphetamines is not yet clear. However, the fact that very large doses can be tolerated by intravenous injection suggests that this is due to a change in the response of the nervous system itself, rather than an increase in the rate of metabolism (chemical inactivation) of the drug in the liver. Since less than half of any administered dose is normally metabolized in man(2), it seems hard to believe that there could be a sufficiently great increase in metabolism to remove the drug rapidly enough to prevent it from acting on the brain. Moreover, tolerance develops more rapidly to some effects than to others: the appetite-decreasing effect wears off earlier than the stimulating action on behavior(58). This must indicate different rates of tolerance development in different parts of the brain.

Despite the apparent increase in tolerance in the nervous system itself, the signs of physical dependence as revealed by a withdrawal reaction are relatively mild. As a rule, the user coming off amphetamines experiences a severe depression and may sleep for several days(9, 29). When he wakes up he has a ravenous appetite, much more than can be explained simply by the length of time he has gone without food(38). These symptoms, as one would expect, are the opposite of the nervous overstimulation and inhibition of appetite produced by the drugs themselves. In the past, most observers have not felt these symptoms to be evidence of a "genuine drug withdrawal reaction". For some reason, many people appear to believe that any drug withdrawal reaction should resemble that caused by morphine withdrawal, regardless of the type of effect the drug itself initially produces.

TYPES OF WITHDRAWAL REACTIONS

If we bear in mind that the withdrawal reaction is probably a result of overcompensation of the nervous system to the drug, then there is no reason to expect that a stimulant drug, such as amphetamine, should give rise to the same kind of compensation or adaptive change as a depressant drug such as morphine. Therefore, it makes no sense to expect a morphine-type withdrawal reaction after chronic use of amphetamines(29, 40).

It is worth noting that the severity of the withdrawal reaction after stopping the drug is not necessarily related to the severity of the dependence. A somewhat oversimplified explanation can be given in the form of an analogy. Suppose that you have to go through a door you are familiar with, and that from past experience you automatically push on the door with the right amount of force to open it. Suppose now that the hinge has become very rusty and you have to apply extra force. The rust can be compared to the effect of an inhibitory drug, and the extra force applied to the door is analogous to the compensatory overactivity of the nervous system. Suppose now that, without your knowledge, someone removes the resistance by oiling the hinge; this can represent abrupt drug withdrawal. If you are unaware of this and push with the greater force to which you have become accustomed, you may go flying through the door. This represents the withdrawal reaction. Suppose, instead, that someone applies a tiny amount of oil each day for several days, so that the hinge gradually loosens. This is analogous to gradual withdrawal of the drug, and you have a chance to re-adapt the pressure of your push in keeping with the changing requirement, regardless of how stiff the hinge was at its worst.

Morphine disappears rapidly from the body when its administration is stopped(14). Amphetamine disappears fairly slowly(58). These facts probably account, to a considerable extent, for the difference in severity of the withdrawal reactions. Unfortunately, there has been a general tendency to think that opiate dependence is a serious problem because the withdrawal reaction is dramatic and severe and that amphetamine dependence is unimportant because on withdrawal the user just goes to sleep. This is a very narrow basis of assessment. As we have noted on page 61, the actual effects of continued heavy *use* of the amphetamines can be much more injurious than those of continued *use* of morphine.

Indeed, the most serious withdrawal reactions are those caused by removal of alcohol or of certain barbiturates, such as amobarbital (Amytal) and secobarbital (Seconal)(26). The full-blown picture of delirium tremens in alcoholics, or the almost identical state that can occur on withdrawal of barbiturates, includes delirium, sleeplessness, tremor, nausea, and convulsions. This reaction has been fatal in numerous cases; the proportion of deaths among alcoholic patients with the full picture has ranged from 2 to 15% in different clincs(4, 60). In contrast, death is very rare during morphine withdrawal reactions. Amphetamine withdrawal has, in a few instances, been followed by suicide during the severe depression which may occur.

CROSS-TOLERANCE TO HALLUCINOGENS

Tolerance to high doses of LSD develops extremely rapidly(8). In general, if LSD is taken more often than once a week the tolerance becomes so marked that the drug soon produces little effect. Three or four successive daily doses are sufficient to abolish the effect completely. When this occurs, the subject is also tolerant to mescaline and psilocybin(19). Since the three drugs are chemically distinct, it might appear that this so-called *cross-tolerance* must reflect an adaptive change in the brain which renders it less sensitive to the similar effects produced by all three. However, metabolic tolerance cannot be ruled out. Even though the three drugs are chemically distinct, certain portions of the molecule are the same in all of them, and it is possible that they are inactivated by the same mechanism. There does not appear to be any recognizable withdrawal syndrome after use of these drugs is stopped. It is interesting to note that tolerance to LSD is not accompanied by cross-tolerance to cannabis(27, 55).

TOLERANCE IN CANNABIS USERS

Many people have stated quite categorically that no toler-

ance or physical dependence are produced by chronic use
of cannabis. In fact Ludlow, a young American drug-user
who was also a very astute observer, pointed out over 120
years ago that the beginner gets *more* effect, rather than
less, each time he uses the drug(31). This phenomenon has
recently received much publicity under the unfortunate
name of "reverse tolerance"(61). It should be emphasized
that this occurs only during the first few times the drug is
used. After that, there is a fairly stable and predictable
effect, according to the amount used. Scientists are not
certain whether the effect initially increases simply because
the novice learns what effects to look for and recognize(1),
or because there is a change in the way the THC is distrib-
uted and handled in the body(22, 43).

With chronic *heavy* use, the available evidence (which
has been accumulating fairly rapidly) suggests that tolerance does develop, so that the user has to take more
cannabis to get the same effect. The Report of the Indian
Hemp Drugs Commission (a widely praised report(32, 33)
by a mixed British and Indian commission which examined
the use of cannabis in India during 1893-94 in a manner
similar to the working of the LeDain Commission in Canada
today) contains evidence that heavy users of bhang, a
preparation of cannabis taken by mouth, needed more
than four times as much drug as moderate users to get the
same effect. Similar observations have recently been
made(57) on heavy marihuana smokers in the Haight--
Ashbury district of San Francisco. In one earlier experimental study(63), human volunteers took pyrahexyl (a potent
synthetic compound closely resembling THC) by mouth,
several times daily for a month, in doses of their own
choosing. There was a tendency for them to increase the
dose slowly but steadily throughout the experiment. In a
similar experiment in which marihuana was smoked, there
was a similar increase in the amount used. Many years ago it
was found that dogs became tolerant on repeated dosage
with cannabis extract(18). A number of very recent studies
in rats(49, 55), dogs(19), and pigeons(5, 47), in which

rather high doses of THC were given, also indicate that tolerance can develop during repeated administration.

CANNABIS AND PHYSICAL DEPENDENCE

The evidence is less complete in relation to physical dependence. One might expect that if it did occur, a characteristic withdrawal reaction would have been recognized in those countries in which prolonged and heavy use of cannabis has existed for centuries. No such reaction has been reported, but it must be remembered that even delirium tremens was not recognized as an alcohol *withdrawal* reaction until fairly recently.

The recent evidence(43) that THC is eliminated from the human body very slowly makes it likely that, as with amphetamine, withdrawal symptoms would be relatively mild even if physical dependence did occur. However, the question does not appear to have received very adequate study so far. In the pyrahexyl experiment mentioned above, the supply of drug was cut off abruptly and the subjects became restless and unable to sleep, sweated heavily, felt "hot flashes", lost their appetite, and had difficulty swallowing. These symptoms suggest a withdrawal reaction, but it is difficult to be sure because the same symptoms could be produced by anxiety or tension resulting from the sudden removal of the drug to which they had become accustomed. In the related experiment with marihuana, similar symptoms did not appear on withdrawal of the drug. These studies are not nearly complete enough to permit any certainty about the occurrence of physical dependence on cannabis.

TOBACCO AND PHYSICAL DEPENDENCE

There is some evidence to suggest the possibility that even tobacco may produce a very mild degree of physical dependence(17, 36).

In one experiment, a large batch of tobacco of very low nicotine content was divided into two lots, and extra nicotine was added to one of them to bring the content up to the range of normal tobacco. Cigarettes of identical appearance were made from the two lots of tobacco, packed similarly, and identified only by code numbers which were kept secret until the end of the experiment. The subjects were given a stock of cigarettes each week, made from either the normal or the low-nicotine lots of tobacco, but they did not know which was which. They were asked to record the number of cigarettes smoked each day, as well as their symptoms. Some smoked a good deal more when given the low-nicotine variety, apparently in an unsuccessful attempt to achieve the effects which they were seeking. At the same time, being deprived of the nicotine, most of them experienced a number of mild physical symptoms which disappeared promptly when they were given a new batch of cigarettes made with the normal nicotine-containing tobacco.

DEGREES AND TYPES OF PHYSICAL DEPENDENCE

If this finding can be corroborated, it suggests that physical dependence can be of very widely differing degrees of severity, as well as of qualitatively different types, according to the drugs used. Therefore, just as in the case of the drug effects themselves, one must remember the importance of quantity as well as quality in talking about physical dependence. It is not enough to ask whether a drug can produce physical dependence; one should also ask *what kind* of physical dependence, and *how severe?*

5

Psychological Consequences of Chronic Drug Use

ORGANIC PSYCHOSES

Probably the most obvious and least controversial psychological consequence of chronic drug use is a psychological manifestation of physical damage to the brain that is referred to medically as *organic psychosis* or *organic brain syndrome*. Organic psychosis is well known in relation to chronic alcoholism(12). It is seen in badly deteriorated alcoholics who suffer from loss of memory, impairment of thought, and inability to learn. As mentioned in the preceding chapter, this condition may result largely from nutritional deficiency related to alcoholism. It does not seem to be common in chronic heavy users of barbiturates, probably because they usually continue to eat well(6). Another possible factor in the production of these conditions is head injury. Alcoholics have a much higher rate of physical injuries, including falls, fights, and automobile accidents(13, 15, 16, 18), than the rest of the population. To some extent, this applies also to barbiturate users.

A further factor, which has not been well explored, may be the production of brain damage by periods of inadequate oxygen supply when breathing is depressed during deep intoxication.

A number of psychiatrists have recently reported the occurrence of what may be a similar organic brain syndrome among some chronic heavy users of cannabis(4, 7, 18), and LSD(1, 3). The symptoms include slowness of thinking, loss of recent memory, vagueness and confusion, difficulty in forming abstract concepts, and changes in the electroencephalogram. They are less marked than those in well-developed cases of brain damage in alcoholics, and so far they have not been definitely proven to be due to damage to brain cells. This can only be ascertained by microscopic examination of the brain at autopsy, and information of this type is not yet available.

Even if brain damage is eventually proven to occur in some users of cannabis and the other hallucinogens, it will still be impossible to be certain, on clinical grounds alone, whether the damage results directly from the action of the drugs, rather than from some other aspect of the living habits of the people who use them. Further clinical observation may be of some help in answering the question, but it will not answer it completely. For obvious ethical reasons, the matter cannot be settled by doing long-term experiments on human beings.

It was noted long ago (5) that dogs given large doses of cannabis daily over many months appeared to become "stupefied". It should now be possible to test pure THC in animals over long periods of time, while keeping the food intake and general hygiene normal, to see if the drug itself causes any brain damage. The lack of such effects in short-term experiments on humans (21) is of no relevance; one would hardly expect to find them. Years of careful clinical observation are required, and until such information is accumulated there is no justification for categorical statements either that cannabis causes such damage or that it is harmless.

PSYCHOLOGICAL DEPENDENCE

One of the most confused areas of discussion concerning non-medical drug use is that relating to *psychological dependence* and *addiction*. The confusion arises from the fact that a great many people use these terms without being very sure about what they mean. Even experts in clinical and research aspects of the subject often use the terms in different senses. One reason for the disagreement is that ideas have been evolving at a fairly quick pace over the past twenty years, as patterns of drug use have been changing rapidly all over the world. As a result, the Expert Committee on Drug Dependence set up by the World Health Organization (WHO) has amended its definitions (and even its own official name!) several times. But many people have continued to use the older definitions and the ideas which these definitions reflect.

For a long time a distinction was drawn between what was called *habituation* and *addiction*(22). There were a number of points of differentiation between these two terms, but the most important were (*1*) that tolerance and physical dependence were an important part of the picture of addiction, but not of habituation; (*2*) that addiction was said to be characterized by an intense craving for the drugs in question, which would lead the addict to try to get them by any means at his disposal, legal or illegal, while habituation was said to give rise only to a moderately strong desire for the drug, but not to compulsion; and (*3*) that addiction was said to give rise to damage not only to the drug user himself but to the people around him and society at large, while damage, if any, produced by habituation applied only to the drug user himself. However, as more and more observations were accumulated about the patterns and consequences of the use of many different drugs in all parts of the world, it became apparent that the distinction between habituation and addiction was a completely artificial one.

There seems to be a continuous gradation of intensity

between very mild discomfort in the absence of the drug, and an intense craving and full-blown physical withdrawal reaction. While some drugs are more typically associated with one pattern of dependence than another, the lines are not sharply drawn; the individual personality seems to have as much influence as the drug in question in determining how severe the dependence is. This point is dealt with more fully on pages 76 to 79. For this reason, the Expert Committee of the WHO(23) finally recommended that the terms *addiction* and *habituation* should be replaced by the single term *drug dependence*, which could include psychological and physical components in varying degrees. They recommended that one should add a qualifying phrase to describe the type of dependence, such as dependence of the morphine type, dependence of the alcohol type, and so forth.

PSYCHOLOGICAL vs PHYSICAL DEPENDENCE

There is a widespread and mistaken belief that psychological dependence is not particularly serious, while physical dependence is. Many people say, for example, that you can be psychologically dependent upon television, upon newspapers, upon morning coffee, upon chewing gum, or upon a whole host of other things which do not have particularly harmful effects upon the user. Therefore, according to this argument, psychological dependence is not really of any importance. In contrast, if physical dependence can give rise to a withdrawal reaction such as delirium tremens, which can be so serious as to kill a certain percentage of its victims, then physical dependence must clearly be very important.

This argument is fairly easily shown to be absurd. Provided the subject survives the acute stage (which he does in the great majority of instances), even the most severe physical dependence fades away fairly rapidly after the removal of the drug. The cellular changes in the brain and other tissues which gave rise to tolerance and to physical dependence gradually reverse themselves, and in a few weeks time at most the subject is again functioning quite normally in the absence of the drug. In other words, the withdrawal reaction may be severe, but it is a short-lived phenomenon which clears up fairly readily. In contrast, psychological dependence can be extremely difficult to eradicate. Drug users show a strong tendency to return to their drugs even after being off them for considerable periods of time. The psychological factors giving rise to drug use, in such cases, are likely to continue in operation indefinitely unless an addict can change his entire living pattern and his manner of thinking and feeling. Therefore, it is the degree of psychological dependence which really determines the importance of drug use in his life and consequently the degree of disturbance which it is likely to produce for him.

A MODERN PSYCHOLOGICAL THEORY

The reason is best explained by outlining a psychologist's view of the nature of psychological dependence and how it is produced(15). In Figure 2 we can picture the individual as being initially in a balanced "neutral" state in which he has minimal wants or needs and can be considered satisfied or at rest. If we now assume that some disturbing factor is applied to him from either the outside or within his own body such as to upset this neutral state, our subject is said to experience a *drive state*. The stimulus giving rise to this drive state can be something quite simple and instinctive, such as hunger, thirst, sexual drive, or the need to escape from a sudden danger or threat. The stimulus may also be something much more sophisticated and elaborate, such as frustration in work, social aspirations, feelings of inadequacy, or depression arising from one's relations with other people. It may be something as mild as simply feeling a little awkward on coming into a party and not yet being involved in the conversation and the activities of the others present. Whatever the reason for the drive state, it expresses itself by stirring the person into some kind of action.

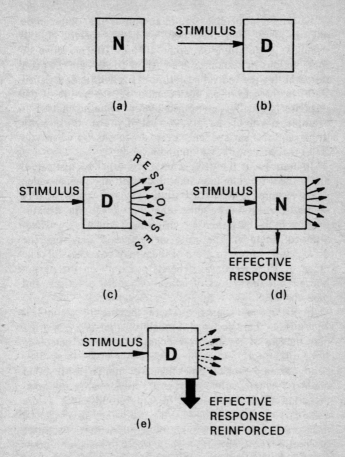

Fig. 2 *Schematic explanation of the formation of behavioral patterns, including drug dependence. (a) Subject is in neutral state. (b) Stimulus disturbs him, creating drive state. (c) This leads to a variety of responses. (d) One of these successfully relieves drive state. (e) With each such success, this particular response becomes increasingly more probable and prompt, displacing other responses.*

As shown in the diagram, the responses or actions can be one or many, and they may be highly specific to the stimulus in question or rather diffuse. The objective of these actions or responses is somehow to alleviate the drive state and let the individual return to his neutral or satisfied state. In the case of an instinctual drive, the nature of the response is usually determined by the same instincts. For example, if you are hungry, you eat; if you are thirsty, you drink; and if a car suddenly bears down on you when you step off the sidewalk, you jump back.

In contrast, if the drive stimuli are rather sophisticated, and if the drive state is a rather ill-defined one such as vague anxiety, unrecognized frustration or aggressiveness, apathy or mild depression, or some other state of general dissatisfaction, then the responses can be many and widely varied. Some of them will be quite ineffective in alleviating the drive state, but one or more of them may be successful. The range of such responses depends not only on the person himself but on factors of education, social practices, and pure chance.

In groups or countries where the use of alcohol is widespread, there is a high probability that taking a drink may be one of the many responses made by a person in some discomfort, simply because it is one of the things that people around him do and encourage him to do. In other countries, where different drugs are used, chance will favor his using these other drugs. In some groups, such as the adherents of certain religions, the use of any psychoactive drug is strongly disapproved, and people with similar types of emotional discomfort are more likely to react with other types of behavior. The role of example, social pressure, and availability, as we explained in Chapter 3, is thus to determine to some degree the range of responses which the person may make.

A response that is successful in alleviating the drive state is said to be *rewarding*. The next time the drive state arises, the subject is more likely to make that response than to make the others. The effective response is then said to be *reinforced.* The more often the same factor gives rise to the same drive state and the same response successfully relieves it, the more strongly entrenched that particular pattern of response becomes.

The particular response or responses which are reinforced may vary according to the individual, even if the drive state is much the same. For example, one person may respond to anxiety or frustration by eating. If this alleviates his discomfort, he will begin to react regularly to such discomfort by eating. This type of neurotic overeating is at the basis of many cases of severe obesity. Another person may react by using a psychoactive drug, and for the same reason he may develop an almost automatic pattern of drug-taking when he is subjected to the situations which give rise to his discomfort. The one person is said to be psychologically dependent upon excess food, while the other is psychologically dependent upon drugs. The meaning of the term is that if they do not have the food or the drugs available when they are subjected to the discomfort-producing stimuli, they do not have other suitable methods or responses available to alleviate the discomfort and so they feel varying degrees of additional distress. The intensity of this distress will vary with the severity of the drive state and also with the degree to which the people in question have become self-trained to use the food or drug response instead of other possible measures.

The speed with which a particular response succeeds in reducing the level of discomfort has an important bearing on how strongly it is reinforced. As we noted in Chapter 2, narcotics which are injected into a vein produce intense effects within minutes, while the same drugs act somewhat less quickly when smoked and much more slowly when taken by mouth. The same holds for injection versus swallowing of amphetamines(9). Therefore, the connection between the drug injection and the change in mood produced by the drug is much more obvious and the reinforcement greater. This is why psychological dependence develops much more rapidly and is much greater in strength in the case of injected drugs than of other drugs (or even the same ones) taken in other ways.

Sometimes the dependence is at least partly on the act of injection rather than on the drug itself. By association with the drug effect, the injection itself can become a rewarding response. Some people feel a strong need to inject almost anything, even substances which have no known drug effect. These people are often, and appropriately, called "needle freaks". In a comparable way, the strong dependence on cigarettes, and the great difficulty in giving them up, may be related in part to the immediate gratification produced by the *act of smoking*, rather than by the *drug action* of the nicotine.

MILD OR SEVERE DEPENDENCE

From the above model it is easy to see why there can be psychological dependence upon a wide variety of different substances or habits, and why the dependence can be mild or severe. If the dependence is basically rather mild and upon a substance or practice which is not particularly harmful in itself, then psychological dependence is not of any great consequence. On the other hand, if the dependence is strong and is centered upon a substance or practice which can give rise to serious physical damage or social injury then psychological dependence is a serious problem. *It is not the presence of dependence itself which is the problem; it is the severity and consequences of that dependence which are important.*

THE ROLE OF THE SETTING

The creation of this type of *conditioned behavior,* of which drug dependence is a specific example, usually depends fairly heavily upon characteristics of the setting in which the reinforced response is made. For example, an alcoholic may have acquired a psychological dependence on drinking in a particular setting, with a certain group of companions in whose company the drive stimulus originally arose (for example, a group of tavern "regulars"). He may feel little or no need to drink when he is removed from that setting — for example, if he is placed in a hospital for treatment of alcoholism. As long as he is in the hospital or in some other protected environment in which the initial drive stimuli and the associated stimuli of his usual company and surroundings are absent, he may feel no need whatever to drink. However, on leaving the hospital and returning to his former company and surroundings, he may immediately experience a strong need to drink. This will be because a secondary drive state has been created by the setting itself.

In the same way, if an alcoholic has previously been physically dependent and has learned to drink in order to alleviate the alcohol withdrawal symptoms, these symptoms may become effective as drive stimuli in their own right. They are not particularly specific symptoms. They could be produced by other types of physical distress or illness or by excessive anxiety. Therefore, if they should arise from these latter causes, they may provoke a renewed drinking response, just as if the alcohol withdrawal state were present. This is probably one reason for relapse into renewed drinking when the person has been successfully off alcohol for some time. Exactly the same considerations apply to the creation of dependence on all other types of psychoactive drugs, including tobacco.

EFFECTS ON PERSONALITY DEVELOPMENT

From this description of the production and significance of psychological dependence, it should be fairly clear that the development of a reinforced response such as drug-taking means a simultaneous decrease in other types of response which might otherwise have been provoked by the same drive state. This means that as drug-taking becomes more and more firmly established, the total range of responses which a person might make to disturbing stimuli is gradually restricted. This is a loss, because some of the alternative responses, even though they might be initially less satisfying, might be more useful in meeting similar problems in the future.

For instance, the best response to a situation giving rise to frustration might be the learning of new skills so that the frustrating problem can be overcome. This takes time, effort, and a certain amount of willingness to postpone the immediate gratification or relief of the drive state. If drug-taking produces a more immediate gratification, the incentive to learn the more constructive response is diminished. This may be particularly important during adolescence because this is the stage of life in which the most rapid expansion of skills and patterns of reaction takes place. Many psychiatrists(8, 10, 20) feel that one important consequence of chronic drug use or drug dependence in young people is a reduction in the variety and range of skills which they acquire for dealing with other people and meeting problems of various kinds.

To the extent that this development of personality is blocked as a result of drug taking, the user remains at a more or less immature stage of emotional development and may be permanently handicapped in this respect. Many studies have been made in an attempt to identify an "addiction prone" personality. By and large, these studies have turned up nothing that is common to all drug-dependent people except this tendency toward emotional immaturity and inadequacy of responses to interpersonal problems(2, 8).

It seems rather ironic that heavy use of alcohol should be seen as a sign of virility and that our language should contain such phrases as "holding your liquor like a man" when heavy use may in some cases be a reflection of immaturity.

It is not always possible to be certain whether this type of immaturity resulted from a stunting of personality development because of drug use, or whether the drug use arose as a consequence of lack of personality development, filling the need for immediate gratification in people who did not have other ways of resolving their problems. However, as extensive drug use has become more common among young people, many psychiatrists have had an opportunity to observe the course of personality development in groups of young drug users and non-users of similar age, social status, and educational level. Some are convinced that even if heavy drug use is a *symptom* of an immature or disturbed personality, it may also be an important *contributory* factor in further retarding the process of emotional maturation.

We have already referred in Chapter 4 to one possible outcome of prolonged heavy use of LSD, cannabis, and other psychoactive drugs. This is a state of apathy and neglect of almost all activities except drug-taking. This can be seen as the end result of a narrowing of the range of potential responses to drive states, as the drug-taking response is progressively more and more reinforced. Some writers have referred to this as the "amotivational syndrome"(11), meaning that the subject in this state has insufficient motivation to undertake activities aimed at changing either his own state or that of the society around him. It is perhaps a little easier to understand this condition in terms of the model of drug dependence which we have given above, because one can then see that in the extreme case the victim does indeed still have motivation, but it is all directed toward only one activity, that of taking drugs.

FALLACIES IN COMPARING DRUGS

In much of what is said or written about drug use there is an underlying assumption that the drugs can be ranked on a scale of danger or actual harm. Most people, including most medical men, place the opiate narcotics at the head of the list. They are even considered to be in a class by themselves and are often called "hard drugs" while all others are lumped together as "soft drugs". Because they can cause rapid development of a high degree of tolerance, physical dependence, and a dramatic withdrawal reaction, and because their use is linked (in Western society) with criminal activity, they are seen as the most dangerous group of addicting drugs.

Probably most people would put alcohol next on the list, because of the many cases of liver disease and other physical illness caused by it, its role in automobile and other accidents, its contribution to crime and violence, and its disruptive effects on work and family relations.

At or near the bottom of the list, most people would probably rank the barbiturates and other sleeping pills, tranquillizers, stimulants, and other prescription drugs used for modifying mood. The illness caused by them is not generally known and, in any case, would probably be considered insignificant beside the benefits resulting from their medical use.

Opinions might be more sharply divided about marihuana, "speed", LSD and other hallucinogens. The extravagant accounts of marihuana as a "killer drug", which were believed by many people a few years ago, have now been largely replaced by equally passionate arguments that it is a completely harmless substance that has not been implicated in the production of disease in the way that alcohol has. On this basis, many people would put it at the bottom of the list. Enough has been written about the perils of "speed" and LSD, much of it as lurid and exaggerated as the earlier stories about marihuana, that many people would probably place these drugs somewhere between alcohol and the narcotics, although they might be a little vague about the exact position.

From the scientific point of view, this ranking or hierarchy of drugs is quite inaccurate because it is not based on a single consistent set of criteria. For example, we have already noted (page 68) that withdrawal reactions from barbiturates and alcohol may carry a higher risk of death than narcotic withdrawal does. Similarly, the physical and psychiatric complications of *heavy* use of amphetamines may be more dangerous than those of narcotic use under some circumstances (page 61). We have also noted (Chapter 4) that marihuana is probably not as harmless physically as many people believe and that it has certainly been implicated (page 73) in some types of mental illness. As we shall see later (page 107), the fact that marihuana has been implicated in much less illness than alcohol may be explainable simply on the basis that it has not yet been used nearly as widely or as long as alcohol has in our society.

Besides being incorrect, this ranking of drugs tends to confuse issues by focussing attention primarily upon the drugs rather than upon the people who use them. Many studies have shown that *heavy* users of any one of these drugs are likely to be users of other drugs as well. Even more important, most types of damage due to drugs are more likely with heavy than with light or occasional use. There is little doubt that somebody who smokes twenty pipes of hashish a day for years is much more likely to suffer physical or mental damage than a patient who is given a few injections of morphine after an operation.

At the same time that the Indian Hemp Drugs Commission was conducting its enquiry, a British Royal Commission investigated the use of opium in India(14). They concluded from the medical evidence that "opium is harmful, harmless, or even beneficial, according to the measure and discretion with which it is used." The point to be emphasized is that *the degree of risk is related not so much to the specific drug which is used as to the amount, frequency, and manner of its use.* Comparisons between drugs simply tend to obscure this point, and to that extent they are often misleading. This very important concept will be examined in more detail in Chapter 7.

6
Social Consequences of Chronic Drug Use

WHAT DO WE MEAN BY SOCIAL CONSEQUENCES?

In Chapters 4 and 5 we have dealt with a number of ways in which chronic use of psychoactive drugs may affect the physical and psychological condition of the person who uses them. These are commonly regarded as consequences for the individual alone, rather than for the rest of society. Such a distinction is merely one of convenience for purposes of discussion. It is difficult to imagine any effect on the individual that would have no effect on the rest of society. For example, an illness that requires hospitalization represents an economic cost to the community, as well as competition for a hospital bed that some one else might otherwise occupy. Mental effects that alter one's ability or desire to work may result in hardship for one's dependents or a welfare cost to the community. Many such examples could be given, all of which follow from the fact that "no man is an island." This chapter really deals with social *aspects* of the individual consequences of drug use, rather than with a wholly independent set of questions.

In Chapter 7 we shall be dealing with the problem of evaluating the effects of drug use — of trying to decide whether they are "good" or "bad". Without getting into the details of this problem here, we should point out that there is no reason why all the consequences of chronic drug use must necessarily be "bad" or "harmful". In Chapter 3 we considered the possibility that drug use by some people might be a form of self-treatment, or that it might involve less conflict between them and the rest of society than would result from certain other forms of behavior that might be prevented or replaced by drug-taking. However, most investigators who have examined the social consequences of drug use have been looking for harmful effects, and virtually no systematic study has been made of possible beneficial ones. This should be kept in mind, in reading the rest of this chapter.

DRUG USE AND ACCIDENTS

In the preceding chapter, we saw that the WHO Expert Committee on Drug Dependence had taken account, in their early attempts to define addiction and habituation, of the fact that chronic drug use might give rise to harm not merely to the user but to those about him(36). One of the most obvious examples of such social damage is the occurrence of death, injury, or property damage as a result of accidents in which drug users are involved. A great deal of evidence concerning these has been accumulated from many different countries over a period of years. It indicates that a high proportion of motor vehicle accidents are caused, in part or in whole, by impairment of driving ability as a result of alcohol intoxication(35).

A number of studies, in Canada and elsewhere, suggest that such accidents are much less likely to happen to light or moderate drinkers who might, under exceptional circumstances, become more intoxicated than they usually permit themselves to be. When this happens to a normally moderate drinker he may either avoid driving or drive with extreme caution so as to minimize the impairing effect of his drinking. Alcohol-provoked accidents are much more common among alcoholics. Even though alcoholics make up a relatively small proportion of the total population of drivers and of those who use alcohol, they make up a high proportion of those who drive, while impaired. Their high accident rate has been attributed also in part to the immature personality characteristics of the chronic heavy drinker, which we have already considered(29, 30).

Barbiturates are similarly involved in accidents, injuries, and suicides(16). As we have already noted, there is a good deal of evidence to show that impairment due to alcohol or barbiturates can be enhanced by the simultaneous use of tranquillizers, other sedatives, and anti-histaminics(26). Some very preliminary evidence suggests that amphetamine users may also be disproportionately heavily involved in motor vehicle accidents(16). This information is by no means conclusive but is enough to warrant a closer and more detailed examination.

There is also insufficient information to permit any valid conclusion about the possible effects of cannabis in this respect. Many marihuana users state emphatically that marihuana is safer than alcohol, citing as their evidence a recent paper (9) which reported that a moderate dose of marihuana, enough to produce a "social marihuana high", did not cause any impairment of performance in a simulated automobile driving task, while alcohol did. However, the study in question did not actually provide evidence for such a statement at all. The subjects were all experienced marihuana users, and the dose of marihuana was purposely kept quite small, merely enough to produce a mild feeling of pleasure. In contrast, the dose of alcohol which they were given was equivalent to about eight ounces of whisky to a person of average body weight, and this amount was drunk in half an hour. Any comparison between the two drugs, on the basis of this wide discrepancy in dose, is clearly quite meaningless(13).

Experimental evidence in animals, as well as in humans, suggests that the intensity of effects produced by marihuana increases in proportion to the dose. Therefore it seems highly likely that, with properly performed experiments, it will turn out that larger doses of marihuana do impair performance of the type required for handling a motor vehicle. A very recent study(19) indicates that even a moderate dose of THC smoked by human volunteers caused significant impairment of performance on a task that required precise timing and fine control of muscular coordination.

So far, preliminary investigation suggests that chronic users of marihuana do not commit significantly more violations of traffic regulations than non-users, and that they have not been involved to any greater extent in the production of automobile accidents(20). However, many of these users believe that their driving ability is impaired when they are under the influence of the drug. Because of this, they either do not drive after smoking marihuana or drive extremely carefully. An added reason for their caution is a desire to avoid being stopped by the police, because they are afraid that their use of cannabis might then be detected; they fear the risk of legal penalties in connection with drug use rather than with their driving performance. If marihuana were not illegal, as it is at present, this reason for extra caution would not exist, and therefore a larger proportion of people might drive while under its influence. The possible contribution of marihuana to the production of accidents might then be more significant than it appears to be at present.

Another fact to be remembered, in this connection, is that sensitive, accurate methods of measuring THC in blood or other body fluids are not yet available. This means that under the conditions that might be encountered in automobile accidents it is impossible to prove the presence of THC in the body. This is quite different from the situation with alcohol. Blood alcohol levels can be measured quite readily, either by drawing blood samples for direct chemical analysis or by use of the Breathalyzer test. Therefore the apparent lack of involvement of cannabis in motor accidents at present may merely mean that its role has not been detected.

Accidental deaths have also occurred in connection with the use of other drugs. We have already mentioned deaths occurring as a result of accidents produced by the hallucinatory state following ingestion of LSD(2). Other accidents have occurred in connection with glue sniffing(18). The common practice is to empty a tube of airplane glue or some other volatile solvent into a bag. The user holds this over his face in order to breathe the concentrated fumes. Plastic bags are sometimes preferred to paper bags because they are more impermeable; for this reason, the solvent vapors cannot escape. However, they collapse more readily when the user breathes in the contents of the bag. When he becomes stupefied by the action of the drug, the user may inhale deeply enough to pull the plastic bag over his nose and mouth and thus bring about death by suffocation. Accidental deaths such as these are dramatic. They have received wide publicity in newspapers and elsewhere. But the reported cases are relatively few in number, and there is probably no valid estimate available of the total number which may have occurred.

DRUG USE AND CRIME

There is much less agreement about another claimed consequence of chronic drug use—namely, the production of various types of antisocial behavior, especially crimes of violence. It is very well known, both from court records and from everyday experience, that a certain proportion of people who become intoxicated with alcohol become aggressive and that some of these commit violent acts. The reason for this has been considered in Chapter 2 in connection with the pharmacological effects of alcohol. As we noted there, one of the effects of alcohol is a decrease in the inhibitory control of one's behavior and emotional expressions which is normally exerted in the alert conscious state. It would not be surprising, therefore, if various types of crime were committed more frequently during the intoxicated state.

Since a certain proportion of people at any given time are likely to harbor feelings of resentment and hostility, it is also not surprising that when control over these feelings is decreased by alcohol the expressed feelings may give rise to aggressive behavior. Recently there have been reports of acts of violence committed by users of amphetamines(8). In a number of cases described in medical records, acts of violence by amphetamine users have been due to their reactions against imaginary persecutors who formed part of the paranoid delusions resulting from the amphetamine intoxication(14).

The most striking contradictions occur in relation to the claimed role of cannabis in the production of crime. The Indian Hemp Drugs Commission of 1893-94 concluded that there was no valid evidence that cannabis use was a cause of crime(15, 27). In contrast, law enforcement officials in North America and elsewhere have long contended that the use of marihuana leads to the commission of crimes, especially crimes of violence(11, 23). Many statements of this type are made with no supporting evidence. Lurid reports of murders committed under the influence of marihuana are based on accounts of a very small number of cases such as that of a young man who went berserk and killed other members of his family. There is no clear evidence that the crime was due to the marihuana, since such murders have often occurred as a manifestation of severe psychosis without the use of drugs.

Cannabis has also been blamed frequently as a cause of rape and other sexual offences(23, 24). Concern with this matter is particularly evident in areas where racial segregation is or has been practised and where sexual assaults by black men upon white women have been viewed with special alarm. An interesting example is provided by a South African commission set up to study the use of cannabis a few years ago(28). They found no evidence to support such an effect, and indeed said that cannabis appeared to *reduce* sex drives. Yet their only specific recommendation for scientific research was for study of the connection between cannabis and sex offences, "as this question is of importance to the Union with its multiracial groups." It is clear that ideas or fears of this type, once planted, are not easily eradicated by contrary evidence.

The proponents of legalization of marihuana often argue that this drug does not give rise to crimes of violence because its major effect is to induce a state of passivity and mild euphoria that is most unlikely to generate crimes of any kind, especially crimes of violence. Folklore and hearsay provide such directly contradictory statements as the following: (*1*) the Egyptians were rumored to have been so easily defeated by the Israelis in 1967 because many of their troops were in a state of passivity due to the use of hashish(21); (*2*) the otherwise non-belligerent Malagasy men fought courageously against the French because their officers supplied them with a cannabis preparation which released aggressive behavior(25); and (*3*) the Egyptian government has been attempting for years to eradicate the use of hashish in Egypt because it is said to give rise to so many crimes of violence(22, 32).

Such contradictions may arise for various reasons. One reason is undoubtedly that many statements are made purely on the basis of preconception or bias, without any supporting evidence whatever. Another may be a failure to distinguish between cause and coincidence. Before the present wave of drug use by middle class North American and European youth, drug use was generally considered to be largely confined to lower socio-economic groups, among whom crime rates were generally higher as well. As a result, crimes committed by users of cannabis and other drugs were often attributed to the drugs, without any attempt to analyze the connection between crimes and drugs.

This type of reasoning is well illustrated by the frequent assertion that the use of marihuana leads to heroin addiction. A recent study(1) of all heroin addicts who were admitted to the U.S. Public Health Service Narcotic Addiction Hospitals at Lexington and Ft. Worth during a part of 1965 showed that the majority of heroin users had indeed used marihuana before starting to use heroin, but that the connection was a complex one. In most cases they had begun to use marihuana as a sign of belonging to teen-age gangs in the slums of New York and other big cities. Another part of the gang activities consisted of petty crimes such as theft, gang fights, and similar activities which brought them into trouble with the police and led to jail sentences. In jail they met older men who introduced them to the use of heroin, and they continued this practice after release from jail. In such cases, it would be incorrect to attribute the use of heroin directly to the use of marihuana; it would be a much more accurate statement to say that the use of heroin was a result of having been sentenced to jail.

Another reason for the conflicting claims with respect to the connection between marihuana and crime lies in the definition of what constitutes crime. If it is illegal to possess marihuana, then it follows automatically that anyone who uses it is committing a crime by so doing. It would be incorrect, therefore, to say that marihuana is *causing* the crime; its use *is* the crime. The only meaningful evidence would be the relation between cannabis use and crimes other than possession of, or trafficking in, cannabis. This is a highly complex matter which has not yet been adequately studied(7).

The picture is somewhat different with respect to heroin and other opiate narcotics. Illicit heroin, sold to users through a chain of middlemen and street-level pushers, is usually an expensive drug. In order to maintain his desired level of drug intake, especially when the development of tolerance has led to a much increased drug requirement, a user may have to spend far more on drugs every day than he could earn in an occupation that was within the law.

Consequently, many heroin addicts are guilty of theft, fraud, prostitution, and similar crimes committed in an effort to obtain enough money to continue their drug use at the desired level(17). Here again, one should distinguish between crimes caused by the drug and crimes caused by financial needs involved in obtaining the drug. In Britain, the USA, and other countries, reasonable numbers of narcotic users have been stabilized by the administration of drugs legally provided by a physician or a clinic at minimal cost. The use of the drugs under these conditions does not in itself appear to give rise to crime(12).

With respect to the actual effects of the drugs, it is probable that further experience with widespread use of marihuana will indicate much the same sort of connection as exists between alcohol and crime. In view of the similarities between the effects of *moderate* doses of marihuana and alcohol on emotional control (see Chapter 2), it would hardly be surprising if disinhibition of emotional expression under the influence of marihuana, just as under the influence of alcohol, did not occasionally give rise to overtly aggressive behavior(33). Nevertheless, a number of observers have reported that such behavior may be less frequent with marihuana than with alcohol because of the passivity and lethargy which cannabis is said to produce(3, 4, 5). Some care is necessary in judging these reports because alcohol users include almost the whole range of the adult population in North America while cannabis users still form a minority which may contain a higher proportion of non-violent people (such as "flower children") than the general population.

ECONOMIC COSTS

Because of the very widespread use of alcohol throughout most of the Occidental world and a large part of the Eastern world as well, much attention has been paid to other costs of alcohol use besides crime and accidents. For example, claims have often been made about the cost of impaired industrial productivity caused by absenteeism from work due to intoxication or hangover(34), although such claims are difficult to prove. Other estimates have been made of the cost of hospital care of alcoholic patients, cost of welfare payments to neglected or abandoned families of alcoholics, and the cost of police and judicial operations made necessary by crimes or accidents provoked in one way or another by alcohol.

To some extent, these estimates are misleading. They create the impression that if alcohol use could be abolished these costs would disappear. This is not necessarily true. Many of the people involved have multiple problems, of which their drinking is only one aspect. For example, a substantial number of those sentenced for crimes related to alcohol are also guilty of crimes committed in the absence of alcohol. Abolition of alcohol use might make little difference to the total cost of administration of justice in the case of such people. Moreover, it must be remembered that the legal sale of alcohol brings a very large revenue to the provincial governments. According to one estimate based on the number of alcoholics in Ontario and the average consumption of alcohol by each of them, the province might lose $40,000,000 a year if all the alcoholics stopped drinking(10). It is easier to estimate the costs of illegal narcotic use because this brings in no compensating revenue to the government.

Similar estimates have not yet been made with respect to the social costs of the use of other types of drugs, but there is no reason to believe that the principle is fundamentally different. For example, descriptions from India, Morocco, Egypt, and Brazil indicate that chronic heavy users of hashish and other cannabis preparations constitute a socially derelict group who are in many ways comparable to skid row alcoholics. The question of costs to their respective societies must be considered in the same light as those arising from alcohol. We have referred (page 83) to the "amotivational syndrome" described among young people heavily involved in the use of hashish, marihuana, and other drugs in Canada and the USA. It seems reasonable to expect that as they grow older they too may constitute a drug skid row comparable to the alcohol skid row of previous generations.

Even though LSD is considered a much more potent drug than cannabis because of its dramatic acute effects, it may be less likely to produce this type of long-term change. Because of the rapid development of tolerance to LSD (page 68), it cannot be used much more frequently than once a week. In contrast, the tolerance to cannabis is considerably less marked, and there are now reliable reports of young North Americans who smoke as many as *20 marihuana cigarettes every day*(6, 31). Therefore the cumulative long-term risks of *heavy* cannabis use may possibly prove more significant than those of LSD use.

Even under present conditions, drug use has a substantial social cost, although it has not been accurately measured. Some of the cost is a result of existing drug laws. For example, the direct cost of police operations against drug users and traffickers, the cost of operating courts and penal institutions, and the personal cost to the careers and opportunities of those convicted are directly attributable to the fact that the use of many drugs is illegal. These costs would presumably disappear if the restrictive laws were repealed.

In contrast, other costs arise as a direct result of the drug effects themselves. These include the cost of medical care and hospital facilities for treatment of mental and physical illness caused by drugs and the cost of educational campaigns aimed at reducing the frequency of such illness. Repeal of the drug control laws would probably *increase* these latter costs. Even the expenses of the various provincial alcoholism and drug addiction research agencies and of the LeDain Commission itself represent part of the social cost of drug use.

7

Evaluating the Effects of Drug Use

DRUG EFFECTS – GOOD OR BAD?

In the previous chapters we have reviewed in some detail
the effects characteristically produced by different types of
psychoactive drugs. We have also examined the reasons
offered for the use of these drugs and some of the physical,
psychological, and social consequences of their chronic use.
So far we have limited ourselves to a description of facts
and possibilities, regarding these purely as phenomena
which can be described scientifically and objectively. However, most members of the public are not concerned with
these things merely as scientific data. To most people, drugs
are important because they may exert either a beneficial or
a harmful effect upon the lives of human beings and upon
the function of society as a whole.

The contradictions and misinterpretations which we
have noted in connection with what might be called simple
matters of fact, are minor indeed compared to the violent

arguments which rage over the question of whether certain drug effects are to be considered good or bad. The reason is readily apparent. The classification of any drug effect as either "beneficial" or "harmful" depends on the scale of values of the person who is making the classification.

Some effects provoke very little disagreement. For example, almost everyone agrees that physical injury is bad. Cirrhosis of the liver produced in chronic alcoholics, accidental death from overdose of barbiturates, and embolism produced by the intravenous injection of suspended particles in preparations of cannabis or in opiate preparations unfit for intravenous use are nearly always recognized as bad, even by the users themselves.

In contrast, those drug effects which are manifested primarily in terms of altered behavior are seen in a very different light by those who favor and those who oppose drug use. The reported enhancement by marihuana of the sensual pleasure arising from sexual activity, or its prolongation by amphetamine, are regarded as bad effects by those who consider sexual activity, especially extramarital sex, as intrinsically immoral. On the other hand, those who favor complete freedom of sexual behavior may well find these same drug effects beneficial.

Interestingly, the effects of alcohol and of marihuana in decreasing the degree of self-control over emotional expression are generally regarded as beneficial if they give rise only to a feeling of relaxation and social conviviality, but the same actions are generally regarded as harmful if they release aggressive behavior, giving rise to fighting or crime. Yet even this unmasking of aggressive behavior may be considered beneficial where the circumstances require such behavior, as in war.

The apathy and loss of interest in work and material advancement which have been attributed by some observers to the chronic use of cannabis are regarded as bad effects in most societies. It is often argued that this merely reflects our domination by the "Protestant work ethic"(17). However, this explanation can hardly be applied to countries such as India or Egypt which are certainly not Protestant. It is simply not true that a "work-oriented ethic" is exclusively a feature of Protestant Anglo-Saxon societies. It is an almost universal attribute. The reason is quite simple: most countries, especially those with less social and economic development, require a great deal of hard work by the whole population to achieve the substantial economic gains they desire. Anything that interferes with work is seen to impede the advancement of the society as a whole. In our society, in contrast, the same loss of interest in work is considered praiseworthy by dissenting members who consider that we have become altogether too preoccupied with material ambitions and have fallen victim to "work addiction" or the "rat race".

To illustrate the lack of absoluteness of such value judgments about drug effects, we might even speculate that at some future date in our own society, if automation should ever make work an unnecessary activity for most people, the reduction of competitive behavior and ambition by drugs could be considered socially beneficial.

ESTIMATING THE AMOUNT

It is fairly obvious, therefore, that we are unlikely ever to agree completely on a uniform scale of classification of various drug effects as either beneficial or harmful. However, even if this were possible, there would still remain the problem of estimating the total amount of good and the total amount of harm resulting to a whole society from drug use by its members. If we wish to have a clear picture of the overall significance of drug use, we need some way of estimating how many people derive beneficial effects of all types from drug use and how many people experience the various bad effects.

For some of the effects, reasonably accurate estimates can be made. For example, medical records permit a moderately good estimate of the numbers of alcoholic patients who suffer various complications of alcoholism such as cirrhosis of the liver, peripheral neuritis, chronic brain damage, and other illnesses leading to hospitalization(24). Over the course of time, we will probably gather comparable data with respect to serum hepatitis, various types of malnutrition, and acute psychotic reactions attributable to the use of amphetamines, LSD, and other drugs that are part of the current "scene". Estimates of the roles of different drugs in causing motor vehicle accidents may become more complete and more accurate as further data are gathered.

In contrast, the significance of drug use as a contributory factor in the production of other illnesses may never be adequately estimated. For example, the lowering of resistance to infections such as pneumonia, abscesses, or gastrointestinal infections may be impossible to estimate. These diseases occur frequently in the general population, and the role of drugs is presumably to lower the individual's resistance somewhat by decreasing his attention to personal hygiene or impairing nutrition. It would be almost impossible to assign a quantitative value to this effect of the drug use.

Beneficial effects would be even harder to estimate quantitatively. For example, there would be virtually no records to which we could turn for an indication of how many people clearly derived simple pleasure from the use of alcohol, cannabis, or other drugs during the course of a year. In its Interim Report (5) the LeDain Commission states, on the basis of its public hearings, that most use of psychoactive drugs seems to be motivated simply by desire for pleasure or enjoyment of the drug effects. Assuming this to be true, it might theoretically be possible to do surveys throughout the country in order to find average values for the number of times a week, month, or year each person obtained the desired pleasure. We could find out, at the same time, how many times he was deprived of this by hangover, untoward drug effects, or social mishaps resulting from drug use. However, the difficulty of designing a scale of degree of pleasure is immediately obvious.

If one were to attempt to estimate the beneficial effects that might be claimed by heavy drug users, or by those who know them well, the difficulties would become completely insurmountable. For example, someone who uses alcohol or cannabis or amphetamine for the relief of neurotic anxiety or depression, even if he did not recognize the motive himself, might reasonably be said to be deriving a beneficial effect. However, others might argue that because of using the drugs he fails to seek psychiatric help which might have removed the causes of his neurotic discomfort. The use of drugs, to that extent, might be considered harmful. There is no need to push the absurdity further. It is sufficient to point out that there are some types of drug effect which we shall probably never be able to estimate quantitatively.

EPIDEMIOLOGICAL CONSIDERATIONS

One way out of this difficulty which can help to give us an idea of how the amount of drug use is related to the overall extent of its consequences (even if we cannot identify or measure all these consequences) is provided by an epidemiological* approach that was first applied to the study of alcohol use by a French scientist, Sully Ledermann(12).

Each person's total alcohol intake over the whole year was divided by the number of days in the year to provide an average daily figure, regardless of whether he drank regularly or only in bouts. Also, by expressing the intake in ounces or grams of pure alcohol content, it was possible to lump together wine, spirits, and beer. Distribution curves were then drawn, showing the percentage of the population falling at or above each level of consumption. Figure 3 shows such a distribution curve.

The same form of distribution has been shown to apply in Canada(6), Finland(12), and other countries. In all cases

---

* Originally *epidemiology* meant the scientific study of the spread of infectious diseases through a population. It is now used more loosely to mean the statistical analysis of the distribution of any kind of disease or phenomenon related to public health.

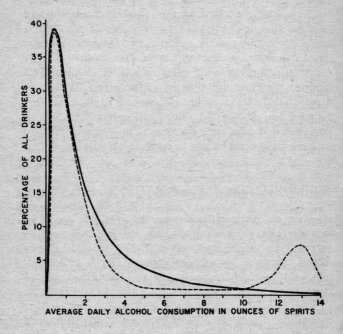

*Fig. 3 Distribution curves showing the percentage of all
    alcohol users at each level of average daily intake of
    alcohol. The broken line (– – – –) shows the type
    of distribution of alcohol intake that would be found
    if alcoholics were clearly different from the rest of
    the population in their drinking habits. The solid line
    (————) shows the type of distribution that is really
    found.*

it was found that the curve of distribution of average consumption per capita showed a continuous smooth fall, from a very large proportion of very moderate users at one end to a very small proportion of extremely heavy users at the other end. It was impossible to recognize any bend or break in this smooth curve which would divide the population into two distinct groups which could be defined as "normal drinkers" and "alcoholics"(6, 12). This is consistent with the results of psychological and biological research concerning the multiplicity of different factors which lead people to use alcohol, the range of different intensities of these causal factors in different people, and the different strengths of psychological reward or punishment which people get from the use of alcohol.

Independently of these studies of the distribution of alcohol consumption, other investigators had examined carefully the minimum average daily intake of alcohol associated with the production of liver cirrhosis and certain other medical complications(14). This level of intake was arbitrarily designated as a point above which drinking could be proven to carry risk of damage to physical health. (This did *not* necessarily mean that drinking below that level carried *no* risks to physical health.) When the frequency of drinking beyond this level was determined for different countries, it emerged that where the degree of social acceptance of alcohol use was high, or where alcohol was more accessible by virtue of a lower price relative to average income, the whole distribution curve was shifted toward the heavier consumption end. Consequently a larger number of users exceeded the minimum level of drinking associated with proven risk of liver disease (Figure 4).

Conversely, where the total use of alcohol by the whole population was less, the whole distribution curve shifted toward the lower consumption end, with a corresponding reduction in the proportion of users who exceeded the level of intake associated with proven risk of liver disease(6, 13, 22).

A very similar result has been obtained in an intensive

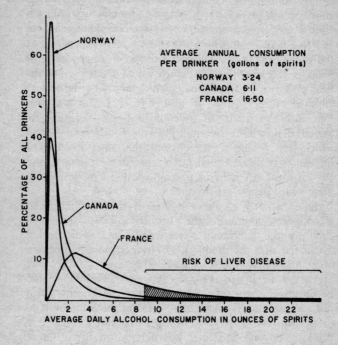

Fig. 4 *Distribution curves for alcohol use in Norway, Canada and France in 1968. The higher the average per capita intake, the more the distribution curve shifts toward the high-intake end of the scale. The hatched area indicates the levels of intake associated with a proven risk of liver disease.*

survey of drug use by over 30,000 Canadian high school students in Toronto, Montreal, and Halifax(26, 27). Each student was asked specifically about his use of each of twelve drugs, ranging from marihuana to heroin, and the number of times per month he used each. The results fell along a frequency distribution curve of the same type we have described for alcohol use. Each drug separately showed such a distribution, as well as the composite curve for all drug use by each student. Just as for alcohol, the comparison of different schools and classes showed that in those where the total drug use was high, the proportion of heavy users was also high. There was also a clear tendency for the heavy users of any one drug to employ other drugs as well.

There is not yet enough valid evidence to permit such a precise analysis of the pattern of distribution of drug consumption in other parts of the world. However, the available information suggests that it also will prove to be similar to that for alcohol(21). For example, it has been estimated that before the Harrison Act was passed in the USA, limiting the sale and prescription of opiates, there were over a million people who used tincture of opium regularly and heavily enough to have signs of physical dependence upon it. Following passage of the Act, which strictly reduced the availability of this drug, use by the whole population decreased drastically and the number and proportion of heavy users also fell sharply(18). This is exactly comparable to the decrease in cirrhosis of the liver when availability of alcohol was restricted by legal prohibition in North America (Figure 5) or by war-time rationing in France (Figure 6) and other countries(3, 10, 13, 20).

Information on cannabis use in other countries is still too sketchy and inadequate to permit the drawing of distribution curves. But in Morocco, where for a time the sale of cannabis was not only legal but was carried on by the government-run tobacco monopoly, the distribution of its use in the population seems to have been rather similar to that of alcohol use elsewhere. There are even reports of

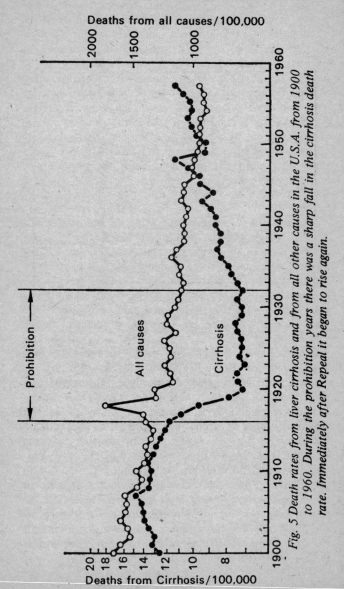

Fig. 5 Death rates from liver cirrhosis and from all other causes in the U.S.A. from 1900 to 1960. During the prohibition years there was a sharp fall in the cirrhosis death rate. Immediately after Repeal it began to rise again.

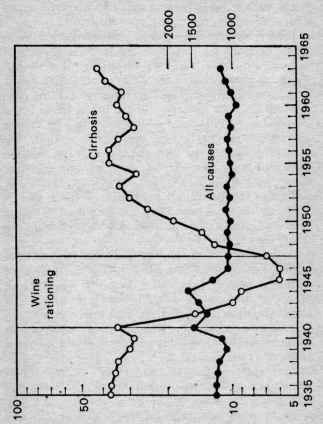

Fig. 6 Death rates from liver cirrhosis and from all other causes in Paris, France, from 1935 to 1965. Wine rationing was imposed during World War II, and was followed by a sharp fall in the cirrhosis death rate. At the end of rationing, cirrhosis rose again to its pre-war level.

extremely heavy and socially deteriorated users of cannabis
in the slums of the large Moroccan cities who are comparable to our own skid row alcoholic population (2, 23).

India is sometimes given as an example of a country in
which cannabis has long been legally available without
any resulting ill effects to the great majority of its people.
This is true, but it must be added that even though cannabis
has been legally available, the great majority of Indians *have
not used it.* Both the report of the Indian Hemp Drugs
Commission in 1894 and the survey reported by Chopra
and Chopra in 1939 indicate that less than 1% of the
population were regular users and that only 0.025% were
considered heavy users. At the same time, over 10% were
regular users of alcohol(4). For comparison, it is worth
noting that about 85% of the residents of Ontario, aged 15
years or older, drink *some* alcohol; 61% drink an average of
at least one ounce of spirits a day, and 5% drink over eight
ounces daily (1968 estimates).

In part, the low use of cannabis in India was due to the
scorn which most Indians felt toward it because of its
association with low-caste users. In part it was due to a
general moderation shown by Indians in relation to all
drugs. Therefore the example of India does not alter the
prediction that an easing of legal restrictions on cannabis in
Canada would be followed by a more rapid increase in the
extent of its use.

These epidemiological observations are extremely important in relation to comparisons of the risks associated with
use of different drugs. As we noted on page 60, many
people in North America believe that marihuana is a much
safer substance than alcohol because it does not cause such
obvious physical damage. This may possibly be true, but
the available evidence does not yet permit any conclusion.
The most recent surveys indicated that up to now only 4%
of adult Canadians have ever used marihuana(8), and that
probably fewer than 20% of high school and university
students in the major cities(26) had used it once or more in
the preceding six months. Corresponding figures in rural

areas and smaller cities are undoubtedly lower.

At a rough estimate, therefore, the number of cannabis users in Canada at that time was probably well below one million at the very most, and the great majority of these were infrequent users who had less than two years' experience with cannabis. In contrast, over 11,300,000 Canadians use alcohol, over 600,000 drink more than eight ounces of spirits daily, and most have made some use of it for several years. A comparable relation between marihuana(15) and alcohol(19) use exists in the USA. Since most cases of alcoholic cirrhosis have had a minimum of five to ten years of heavy drinking before the disease was diagnosed(14), it is obvious that even if marihuana were just as harmful as alcohol we could not possibly be in a position yet to know it.

Another example of the dangers of uncritical approach to statistics is provided by an interpretation placed on certain figures in the Indian Hemp Drugs Commission Report(11), concerning mental illness among heavy users of cannabis. As we noted on pages 38 & 73, certain types of psychosis may be caused or precipitated by cannabis. The Report indicated that during one year, in all of India, only ninety-eight such cases were admitted to mental hospitals. This appears to be a trivial number in a country which had, at that time, a population of about 280,000,000. However, the Commission's enquiry also revealed that during the same year only 1,344 patients were admitted to all the mental hospitals in India. This is an incredibly small figure for such a huge population, and it probably means that the great majority of mentally ill patients were never admitted to hospitals. The important figure, therefore, is not that only ninety-eight cases were admitted with mental illness related to cannabis use, but that *they made up 7.3% of all the patients admitted to mental hospitals in the year.* Since regular cannabis users made up only 0.5% of the population, they must have had a much greater probability of hospitalizable mental illness than the rest of the population(11).

There is another important finding in numerous studies of drug use in Canadian and American cities. As the survey of high school students showed, the heavy users are likely to take many different kinds of drugs(25, 28). Clinical experience with alcoholics shows that many also use large amounts of barbiturates, tranquillizers, and other prescription drugs(7). In a similar fashion, heavy users of marihuana are also likely to take LSD, other hallucinogens, or amphetamines(9, 16, 28). On page 93 we pointed out that there is no evidence for a direct pharmacological connection between the use of marihuana and that of heroin. However, there may be a psychological connection, in the sense that the heavy user, being likely a multiple drug taker already, may be more likely also to try additional drugs, including heroin. One important implication of this finding will come up in Chapter 8, in connection with the role of government in the control of drug use.

As we have seen, it appears that anything which increases the total use of a drug or group of drugs by a large population increases the number of heavy users. It thereby increases the risk of the physical and probably the psychological ill-effects of heavy use, whatever these may be and however difficult it may be to estimate their actual numbers. At the same time, it must be remembered that the reason for the increase in use by the whole population is presumably an increase in the total pleasurable effect which the users obtain. Therefore we can say that in the case of such an increase in overall use the population experiences an increase in total pleasurable or beneficial effects, at the price of an increase in the bad effects of heavy use. Conversely, anything which reduces the whole extent of drug use by the population also reduces the numbers and proportions of those using the drugs heavily and suffering the ill effects. In the latter case, we can say that the potential victims of ill effects are being protected, but at the price of a reduction in the pleasurable use of the drugs by the large number of moderate users in the population.

It is important to keep this epidemiological approach in

mind when one attempts to estimate the significance of governmental intervention in the use of drugs, which we will consider in the next chapter.

8

Role of Government in Drug Use

BASIS FOR LEGISLATION

The Interim Report of the LeDain Commission in Canada(1), the Report of the Indian Hemp Drugs Commission(10), and the Wootton Report in England(9) have all devoted considerable attention to the philosophical basis of government attempts to control or regulate the use of drugs in a society. All these reports have stated clearly and thoughtfully the problem which a government faces in this respect. Essentially it is the choice that we considered at the end of the previous chapter. To what extent should a government allow the widest possible freedom of individual choice and action with respect to drug use, even at the risk of ill effects to some of the people? Conversely, to what extent should the government attempt to protect the people against the consequences of heavy and ill-advised use, even at the cost of a restriction of individual freedom to seek pleasure or other benefits of drug use?

We believe that these questions have been so well dealt with in these reports that it is unnecessary to restate the arguments on both sides. What we are more concerned with here is laying the groundwork for the role of the citizen in this question of decision. We shall attempt to do this by having a more careful look not at the justification for government intervention, but at the ways in which it is actually implemented and what it can and cannot achieve.

HOW DRUG LAWS ARISE

A full summary of the present Canadian legislation on psychoactive drugs and of the international agreements of which Canada is a signatory is contained in the Interim Report of the LeDain Commission(1). Many interesting comments on these laws and agreements are contained in the Interim Report and in Reginald Whitaker's book, *Drugs and the Law*(12). A fascinating account of the origins of these laws is provided in a paper by Shirley Cook(3), copies of which may be obtained from the Addiction Research Foundation of Ontario. We shall not repeat all this information but, rather, confine ourselves to a few observations which are directly relevant to the present discussion.

Drug legislation has arisen in different ways and for different reasons. In Canada the first legislation to control the importation and non-medical use of opium was passed in 1908, at a time when narcotic use does not appear to have been of any consequence except among Chinese immigrant laborers on the west coast. The act was apparently aimed specifically at them and was a response to the concern expressed by a small but active group of anti-opium crusaders which included clergymen, political figures, and members of the Chinese community of Vancouver. In 1911 this legislation was broadened into the Opium and Drug Act, which included cocaine under its controls. This was the result of a campaign mounted by various welfare and religious groups in Montreal, including the Children's Aid Society, which felt that a problem of cocaine abuse existed. No scientific enquiry was held to examine the nature and extent of the alleged problem(2).

In the USA the Harrison Act of 1914 was also a response to the efforts of a group of moral reformers, but in relation to what was seen as a problem in the Philippine Islands. In order to protect the natives against what they viewed as the ravages of opium, a group of American missionaries waged a campaign of moral pressure which led to the prohibition of opium in the Philippines in 1908. In order to obtain the necessary international cooperation to enforce this prohibition, the American government passed an opium control act for the United States in 1909 as a sign of good faith. It also set up a committee to examine the opium situation in the United States, and it was the growing concern of this committee about the widespread domestic use of opium which led to the passing of the Harrison Act. Thus, even though a large number of Americans had been using opium, this was not officially recognized as a "problem" until paternalistic concern for Filipino natives led indirectly to closer self-scrutiny.

The inclusion of marihuana under the Canadian Opium and Narcotic Drug Act of 1923 was not in response to any existing problem, because this substance was virtually unknown in Canada at that time. However, a book which attracted wide attention at the time (8) painted a lurid picture of the moral degeneration which marihuana was said to be producing in some of the larger cities of the United States. Since marihuana was to be discussed at an international convention in Geneva in 1925, the Canadian government decided to include it in the 1923 Act as a precautionary measure.

Although three of the states of the USA had had anti-marihuana laws for some time, the federal government did not forbid the sale or possession of marihuana until 1937. At the time, its use was largely confined to Negro men in the poor areas of large cities and to Mexican and Puerto Rican immigrants.

From this brief historical review, it can be seen that both the Canadian and the American laws against opium and marihuana were initiated by groups which were concerned, on moral grounds, with the practices of foreign peoples or domestic minority groups. These laws were passed on the strength of campaigns based on moral indignation rather than objective examination of statistical or scientific evidence. To the great majority of people in both countries, these drugs were not part of everyday life, and it probably caused them little concern that governments chose to ban substances which they did not use. Present day critics of the laws on marihuana have attacked bitterly the way in which these laws were passed(4, 6, 7, 12). But it must be remembered that moral arguments on such topics were as valid and cogent to the society of fifty years ago as scientific and medical arguments are today. The change in the nature of what we accept as convincing arguments in the health field is simply one more evidence of the way in which society has changed.

The international agreements have a similar history. One drug or another has been proposed for international control on the initiative of a country with special concern about it. Other countries, with no problems of their own because the drug in question was not used by their populations, have generally been willing to agree to the proposed restrictions. Countries in which the drug was used, but posed no serious problem, have not signed the agreements. India, for example, refused for some time to take measures against the use of cannabis because it had a traditional though small role in Indian life and was not considered a problem.

The point we wish to make is that some laws restricting use of certain drugs have been deliberate responses to specific problems, while others were originally proposed by small pressure groups and accepted by an indifferent majority. The legislation as a whole, therefore, *cannot* be regarded as a uniformly well reasoned group of acts based on sound scientific evidence and thoroughly discussed by the public before their enactment. There should be no need, therefore, to regard drug laws as sacred or unchangeable. As the practices and attitudes of our society change, we should be prepared to re-examine these laws if they appear to become inappropriate.

For example, as use of marihuana has become more common in Canada and as pharmacological evidence has shown how unlike the narcotics it is, it is reasonable to ask whether the original decision to include it under the narcotic legislation in 1923 is still appropriate. On the other hand, non-medical use of amphetamines has also become more common and has been associated with serious health problems. For many years amphetamines were under only minimal legal control, despite the close similarity between their effects and those of cocaine, which was under the Narcotics Act. The *omission* of amphetamines might therefore also be considered inappropriate.

Thus, a re-examination of the drug control laws might lead either to the imposition of new restrictions or to the removal or modification of old ones. The important thing is that the existing laws need not be regarded as permanent. The same applies to the international conventions to which Canada has agreed, and it is not very logical, therefore, to argue that Canadian drug laws cannot be changed because of these conventions. The most reasonable course would be to decide first on the appropriate objectives for drug law generally, and the probable effects of specific legislative measures, then to agree on suitable Canadian laws, and only after that to enter into international agreements on these matters.

EFFECTS OF GOVERNMENT INTERVENTION

It is commonly stated, and very widely and uncritically accepted, that government attempts to restrict the use of alcohol, cannabis or any other drug are doomed to failure. The commonly given example is that of prohibition in

Canada and the USA. The statement is made that prohibition was a failure, and that for this reason it had to be repealed. This statement is quite misleading, unless one spells out exactly what prohibition was expected to accomplish and in what way it failed.

If the purpose of prohibition was to abolish *all* use of alcohol, then quite clearly it did fail. Abolition of legal sale of alcohol resulted in the creation of the bootleg alcohol trade, which not only provided users with substantial amounts of badly-made and expensive alcohol but also created a breeding-ground for bootlegging rings which many believe to be the origin of organized crime in North America.

On the other hand, if the purpose of prohibition was to *reduce* the consumption of alcohol, the epidemiological data which we mentioned in the previous chapter show quite clearly that it succeeded, without any question whatever. The total consumption of alcohol decreased drastically. Similarly, the proportion of the population suffering the physical, and presumably the social and psychological, ill effects of excessive alcohol use was drastically diminished. As soon as repeal was instituted, the death rate from liver cirrhosis began to climb steadily to its previous levels (Figure 5).

The proper question, therefore, with respect to legal prohibition of alcohol or drug use, is not whether it is bound to fail, but what it will achieve that is desirable and what it will achieve that is undesirable. In the example that we have just considered, the desirable effect was the reduction of physical damage produced by excessive intake of alcohol. The undesirable effects included a restriction of the individual citizen's freedom to drink as he wished, the creation of a black market in illegal alcohol, and other social ill effects resulting from this.

The effects of narcotic control legislation in Canada and USA can be looked at in the same way. As we have already noted (page 105), this legislation had the desirable effect of drastically reducing the number of people who were seriously dependent upon opiates. On the negative side, however, it created a new class of criminals in relation to the illegal sale and use of narcotics.

In the same way, if the government wished to achieve a substantial reduction in the consumption of other drugs, it could quite probably succeed in this goal by enacting and enforcing sufficiently drastic measures. The question would then be whether the net benefit obtained from reducing the number of heavy drug consumers was worth the cost in socially undesirable consequences of severely restrictive legislation.

One of the social costs of such restrictive legislation which has been pointed out by many concerned people, including the members of the LeDain Commission, is the potential harm to the lives and careers of young people who may be sentenced to prison for possession of illicit drugs. Another, as we have already noted, is the actual monetary cost of maintaining a substantial level of police activity, of conducting judicial proceedings, and of operating penal institutions devoted to the enforcement of restrictive laws against drug use. So far, these monetary costs have not been estimated accurately, but it is important that such information be gathered.

Another of the possible "costs" of governmental restriction of drug use which is often advanced as an argument in favor of legalization of such use is the loss of respect for the law and for law enforcement agencies which is said to result from the enactment of unenforceable legislation. According to this argument, if legal restriction of drug use is obviously a failure and many people know that there is a reasonably good chance of being able to break such laws without risk of penalties, then the public will lose respect for the whole political system which generates them. The same loss of respect is said to ensue if punishment of offenders is erratic, resulting in heavy sentences for a few offenders and none at all for the rest. This argument may have some validity where a government adopts a position which is neither libertarian nor strongly repressive, but in between. Government repression of drug use probably can work if the penalties are made severe enough, and in that case the argument would not apply. However, the problem would then be one of attempting to assess whether the benefits resulting from reduction of heavy use of drugs were worth the price, in the sense which we have already discussed.

THE SUBSTITUTION THEORY

Many advocates of the removal of legal restrictions on the use of marihuana and other drugs argue that present laws tend to drive young people toward the use of more harmful drugs by penalizing the users of marihuana. The assumption is that a need is felt by young people to "do their own thing", and that this involves assertion of their independence by using a drug other than alcohol. If marihuana is denied them, it is said, they will turn to LSD, amphetamine, or narcotics.

A few people have offered the opposite argument in support of continued prohibition of marihuana. If the real need of young people is to assert their defiance of adult society by breaking its laws, says this group, then we should let them continue to break the law on marihuana rather than on drugs which may prove more harmful to them.

Both of these arguments are based on the fallacy that a person is likely to use only one drug and that a second drug is adopted *by substitution for* the first rather than *by being added to* it. We have already seen that this is not true. Wider use of maihuana seems to have been accompanied by increase, rather than decrease, in the consumption of alcohol by the young(11). The great majority of LSD and "speed" users also use marihuana and other drugs(5, 13). It seems fairly clear that use of any psychoactive drug increases the probability of use of other psychoactive drugs. The role of government, therefore, can not be discussed usefully in relation to the control of any one drug, but only in relation to drug use in general.

PUBLIC ATTITUDES AND LEGISLATION

The success or failure of government intervention probably depends principally upon the degree to which the government's action reflects the attitudes and aspirations of the country as a whole. For example, the most important cause of adult mortality in North America today is cardiovascular disease (including hypertension and arteriosclerosis). According to most current scientific thinking, an important factor in the production of these diseases is the consumption of a diet with too much fat, especially of fat with saturated fatty acids, such as those found in meats and dairy products. Theoretically, the government might decide that it should protect the rather large number of people who run a serious risk of heart disease, even at the cost of interfering with the personal freedom of other people, by setting maximum legal limits on the fat content of dairy products and other foods or by rationing them so as to reduce the consumption. Most governments have not attempted such legislation, even though it might be medically beneficial, because it might be strongly resented by the majority of the population.

Similarly, most scientists now agree that there is convincing evidence concerning the role of tobacco in the production of heart and lung disease, including lung cancer. But the Canadian government has not yet attempted to forbid the sale or use of cigarettes, though it is considering the restriction or banning of cigarette advertisements on television. The government of the USA has already taken this latter step. This represents a situation in which the public, while probably unwilling to accept the restriction of personal choice with regard to cigarette smoking, is nonetheless sufficiently worried about the medical hazards of smoking to accept some control over the promotion of tobacco sales.

A third case is that of the fluoridation of public water supplies for the sake of minimizing the frequency of tooth decay, especially among children. Since the addition of fluoride to the drinking water supply does not give rise to any detectable change in the odor, flavor, or color of drinking water, the imposition of this form of compulsory medication does not result in any detectable change in daily life which the public might see as an interference with personal freedom. In contrast, marked reduction of tooth-ache and costs of dental care are clearly a recognizable gain. In this case, therefore, the majority of citizens are prepared to accept governmental intervention, even though a minority view it as an indefensible infringement upon their freedom.

These examples suggest that a government can restrict the freedom of action of individuals where it believes such restriction to be to the benefit of the public as a whole. They also indicate that such restrictive intervention *can* work; that it *will* work if the measures adopted by the government to enforce it are sufficiently strict and are supported by a substantial portion of the public. Finally, these examples indicate that a government is most likely to take such steps where it believes that the public is essentially in sympathy with the objectives.

In the case of drug use, the problem is precisely that the public at large is uncertain about the positions which it takes or should take, and government reflects this uncertainty with respect to its legislative goals. It is therefore of major importance that the public at large should undertake to clarify its own views so that government may reflect this clarification in its actions. In the next chapter, we shall attempt to see exactly what is involved in this matter of clarification.

9

Drawing a Balance

WHAT HAS TO BE BALANCED?

In Chapters 7 and 8, we have talked repeatedly about the need·to balance "good" versus "bad" in several different connections. We have talked of balancing beneficial versus harmful drug effects, benefits of protection versus benefits of freedom, benefits of governmental control versus ill effects arising from the control measures themselves. Before attempting to draw an overall balance sheet as individuals, we should remind ourselves of precisely what kinds of things we are attempting to balance.

Some of the things which we have to balance can be classed as facts. These were the things which were reviewed in Chapters 2 to 6: the effects of drug use, both "beneficial" and "harmful", to the extent that we can agree on these designations. The second set of things which we are attempting to balance are scientific estimates of numbers — the numbers of those who might experience bad effects arising from excessive drug use, versus the numbers of those who would experience beneficial or pleasurable effects from moderate drug use. For the purpose of making this balance, we must either be prepared to accept very rough estimates, so that we can proceed with our balance sheet now, or to postpone any attempt at balance until we have gained a great deal more information. In the latter case we should also be prepared to reckon into the total balance the benefits and harms resulting from a continuation of the *status quo*.

The third type of thing which we have to balance is a set of purely subjective values which depend upon our own individual background, temperament, and education. These are the relative weights which we attach to different "beneficial" and "harmful" consequences of drug use and of legislative control of drug use. These are things which every citizen has to balance for himself, because probably no two citizens share exactly the same scale of relative values. To work with these, we must pose a variety of balance-seeking questions. For instance, *how much* pleasure and individual freedom with respect to drug use is worth *how much* physical, psychiatric, or social damage to the victims of excessive drug use? The same type of balance of relative values must be attempted in relation to the consequences of legal control of drug use. For example, we must consider *how much* protection of vulnerable drug users against the consequences of excessive use is worth *how much* damage to the lives and careers of *how many* drug users as a result of the imposition of prison sentences for illegal possession or trafficking.

The problem becomes even more complex when we attempt to take into account the economic quantities on both sides of the balance sheet. For example, when the French government under M. Mendes-France became concerned about the relation between alcoholic liver disease and the total consumption of alcohol in France (page 105), it began a publicity campaign aimed at reducing the heavy use of wine and spirits. This campaign promptly ran into resistance and protests from a large part of the agricultural population of France because the production and sale of alcohol products provided an important part of their livelihood. In that situation, the costs of illness and medical care had to be balanced against the costs of subsidizing farmers or developing new sources of income for them.

In view of the extreme complexity of such value judgments and attempts to balance one value against another, it is not surprising that a great many people have felt genuinely perplexed or lost. Under these circumstances, many have fallen back on the hope that someone else will be able to answer the questions for them. One frequently hears the statement that we need much more research on the question of drug use before we try to make up our minds about an appropriate position for the law. It might be well to reflect for a moment about exactly what we can and cannot hope to learn from this research.

THE ROLE OF RESEARCH

The most important thing to keep in mind about the role of research in these questions is that research of any kind deals exclusively with facts. Research may certainly be able to provide us with the answers to some questions. How does a particular drug act? How much of it is needed to produce a certain degree of effect? Does it produce tolerance or physical dependence? What are the physical or psychiatric consequences of chronic or heavy use? How much drug must be taken for how long to produce these effects? It will probably be quite possible to determine by experiment whether a given level of marihuana smoking does or does not affect the ability to drive a motor car safely. It will probably be possible to determine with fair certainty whether LSD use does or does not cause genetic damage. It may be possible to determine whether the psychedelic experience does or does not have definite effects on the level of self-understanding or on artistic creativity, and exactly what its role is in precipitating psychotic episodes. It may also be possible to discover what the probability of either type of occurrence is, in people with different characteristics.

Even where research deals with attitudes or values, it deals with them as facts. For example, sociological research may tell us *as facts* what the attitudes toward drug use are in a given population, or how many people hold which views. It may tell us something about the stated reasons for drug use by different individuals and whether these are really the causes, or only what the drug users themselves take to be the causes or the justifications of such use. In all these questions, the scientist records phenomena as he finds them or as he modifies them by experiment, whether these phenomena are physical events or emotions and attitudes of the people he is studying.

It is obvious that research on drugs and drug-related questions is extremely varied, and it would be naive to think that all of it will help to solve the drug problems that we are dealing with today. Some types of research actually create new problems. It should not be forgotten that many of the psychoactive drugs, such as LSD, amphetamine, and DOM, are synthetic. In other words, they are products of drug research, which has indirectly created new social problems. The scientific literature in which the methods of synthesis and the effects of these drugs are described is available to everyone. Thus, people with some training in chemistry can make use of it to set up illegal chemical plants for producing black-market drugs almost as soon as the methods are described in scientific journals.

Other types of research help the scientist and the physician to understand how drugs produce their typical effects and how some of these can give rise to physical and psychological damage. Eventually this should prove useful in developing methods of treatment to arrest or reverse the damage, just as we have penicillin for infections and insulin for diabetes. However, this may take a very long time. Even though a great deal of knowledge has been gained in the last twenty-five years concerning the effects of alcohol on the liver, we still do not have a specific and effective remedy for alcoholic cirrhosis, much less for alcoholism itself.

If we are to understand all the factors which lead people to use drugs and which influence the amount and pattern of such use, it is not enough to study the drugs and their actions. It will be necessary to devote much more attention to psychological, sociological, and anthropological studies, including careful examination of other times and other cultures than our own. Many North American writers seem to feel that it is a waste of time to look at drug use in India, Morocco, Brazil, or elsewhere, because the findings are irrelevant to drug use in North America today. This is a short-sighted approach which assumes that we are somehow different from all other peoples. During the decade after the end of World War II, a major problem of non-medical use of methamphetamine occurred in Japan(2, 5). This was largely ignored in North America and Europe, until the same problem arose there a few years later. By examining the similarities and differences between cultures having access to similar drugs, we can learn a great deal about what is common to all men and what is unique to each culture with respect to influences on drug use.

For example, the cannabis plant was introduced into Chile in the middle of the sixteenth century by the Spanish colonists to be grown for hemp fibre(4). Even though it has appreciable THC activity, the plant was not used as a drug until two or three years ago, when the practice arose together with jeans, rock music, and long hair in direct imitation of the practices of North American youth(1). Similarly, cannabis has been legally available in India for centuries, but, as we have noted, its regular use was generally looked upon with contempt and was practised by a very small portion of the population. Yet today, we have heard(3), many Indian university students are smoking it, not as a re-affirmation of Indian tradition but in imitation of the North American manner. Clearly, studies of such phenomena can teach us much about motives and social influences on drug use.

What research *cannot* do is tell us whether a given event is good or bad. The scientist himself, as an individual, can tell us whether he thinks that the event is good or bad, but his opinion is no more valid than that of any other citizen presented with the same facts. For example, a physicist may know a great deal more than an ordinary citizen about the nature of thermonuclear reactions, about the energy generated by a nuclear fusion reaction, about the extent of damage which can be created by a nuclear blast of a given size in a given location, or even about the probable consequences to human life of a nuclear war. However, once he makes these facts known to the general public, he is no more qualified than all the rest of the public to decide whether a nuclear war is good or bad. That is a matter which every human being is entitled, and in fact obliged, to decide for himself. Most of the apparent contradictions between scientists which can be so confusing to the public are not really disagreements about fact but differences of value judgment or predictions.

THE ROLE OF EDUCATION

The reason for concern about drug use, as we have noted repeatedly, is the danger of serious harmful effects to a minority of users at the heavy-consumption end of the distribution curve. The majority of users — whether of alcohol, marihuana, opium, barbiturates, or whatever — do not suffer these harmful effects, and derive pleasure or benefit from the drugs. We may well ask, then, why all the discussion about the role of government so far has dealt only with the question of the law — to legalize or to forbid. Why is it not possible to direct education or mental health campaigns toward a reduction of heavy use by people in the danger zone, while leaving the rest free to enjoy a harmless amount of drug use?

Theoretically there are two ways of doing this. The first is to concentrate on the heavy users, giving psychiatric treatment to all who need it and re-shaping the attitudes of those who are not diagnosed as ill. Unfortunately this is simply not feasible, because of sheer weight of numbers. As we noted on page 109, in Canada there are over 600,000 people using potentially hazardous amounts of alcohol, and to these we must add the growing numbers of excessive users of all the other drugs. Given the limited numbers of trained psychiatrists and other mental health experts and the fact that they have to help many other people who have difficulties not related to drug use, there simply are not enough to look after all the problems. On top of this, the rate of cure is still relatively low, so that there is no guarantee that a crash program of personnel training would solve the problem.

The second approach would be to change public attitudes by means of massive education campaigns so that everyone would voluntarily use drugs less, thus shifting the whole distribution curve toward the lower end and reducing the number of people in danger. This approach would permit freedom of choice, while at the same time minimizing the risk to the most vulnerable people. Such a solution would be the ideal one for a democratic society, but unfortunately no one has yet found a way to achieve it. As we have noted in Chapter 3, there are enormous pressures acting in the opposite direction, constantly pushing drug consumption upward. Many groups are attempting to develop educational methods that can reverse this trend, and they deserve strong support from governments and the public. However, a long period of evaluation will be needed before it will be possible to know whether or not a particular set of methods is likely to be successful.

Until effective ways are found to bring about this voluntary change in attitudes, the government really has no effective means of modifying the pattern of drug consumption except by manipulation of price and legal status of drugs.

"COST-BENEFIT ACCOUNTING"

Therefore, when all the relevant information has been acquired by means of research, each citizen will still be in the same ultimate position of having to decide what value he puts on all of the beneficial effects, what value he puts on all of the harmful effects, what value he puts on the protective role of the law, and what value he puts on individual freedom from legal restrictions, and he will still have to draw the balance for himself.

When he does so, he must be very clear in his own mind what the probable consequences of any change in the law may be. We have already seen, from epidemiological considerations in Chapter 7, that if the law is made more lenient and drug use is made easier and more socially-approved, it will almost certainly increase greatly in amount. As a result, the numbers of people suffering the physical and psychiatric consequences of excessive use will increase substantially. That calls for one type of balance, in which the injury to increased numbers of victims of drug use — and the cost of providing adequate treatment facilities for them and social and economic maintenance for them and their dependents—must be balanced off against the extra benefits of moderate drug use which a larger number of people will enjoy. On the other hand, stern suppression of drug use by legal methods would reduce this hazard to the heavy users but create an added price in terms of the legal penalties imposed upon those who fall victim to the laws necessary for the maintenance of drug restriction. This will call for a different type of balance in which the value of the protection for the potential victims of drug use must be weighed against the injury inflicted upon the victims of law enforcement.

Specialists in different fields often tend to give greatest importance to the areas of their own interest. For example, lawyers tend to be more concerned about the problems created by the law, while psychiatrists and physicians tend to be more worried about the psychiatric and medical problems seen in heavy drug users. If the general public is to be able to make a reasonable balance, it is essential for them to be provided with actual numbers. If 1,500 people faced trial on drug charges while 15,000 ran into serious medical problems, the decision would probably be very different from that which would be made if 15,000 faced criminal charges and only 1,500 suffered illness. It is important to have some hard facts on this matter.

In the same way, governments are obliged to balance one set of practical problems against another in evaluating the feasibility of a proposed piece of legislation. Suppose, for example, that the Canadian government were to decide that the balance of scientific evidence and value judgment favors the legalization of marihuana. On one side of its balance sheet on feasibility, it would be able to record the elimination of a set of difficulties which exist at present and which we have already considered: the problems and costs of law enforcement, the alienation of one segment of the population, the encouragement of smuggling and so forth. On the other side, however, it would have to face a whole new set of problems:

Because of the international agreements which Canada has signed, the government cannot now permit the non-medical use of cannabis. Would it attempt to change these agreements?

If it failed to do so, as seems probable, would it withdraw from these agreements?

If it withdrew, would it allow private importation, distribution, and sales in Canada without governmental control or supervision?

If so, would it also turn a blind eye to the smuggling of cannabis *in either direction* between Canada and other countries in which cannabis remained illegal?

If there were official control, as for alcohol, would it be under federal or provincial jurisdiction?

If the government were to set up a marihuana monopoly, how would it guarantee the uniform quality of the material sold?

If marihuana grown under uncontrolled conditions in the Canadian climate proved to be too low in THC content to have appreciable drug effect, would the government set up special cultivation of potent strains grown from imported seeds or large-scale production of synthetic THC?

How would it prevent illicit production in Canada?

What would be the minimum age at which people could legally purchase and use cannabis, and how would the limit be enforced?

What penalties would be incurred through violations of this limit, and how would the alienation of young people by this restriction differ from that produced by the present laws?

All these questions would arise, quite apart from the matters we have already considered in relation to the effect on the total level of drug consumption in Canada and on the incidence of harmful effects of drug use.

One of the most important benefits of trying to work through a balance of all the relevant factors that we have considered is the perspective that is gained in the process. Probably everyone knows the fable of the blind men and the elephant. The subject of drugs and society has been like the elephant; many sincere, passionately concerned, and outspoken people have been, if not blind, at least rather short-sighted, seeing only the trunk, the tail or a leg, rather than the whole elephant to which these belong. They have concentrated on a single aspect such as the legal status of marihuana, or drop-in centres for young drug users, or drug education campaigns in schools and universities. The exercise of assessing *all* the costs and benefits of drug use makes it much easier to see clearly the central problem, the interaction of the many influences which determine attitudes toward all drug use and which shape its pattern, amount, and function in the life of the individual. It then becomes easier to avoid the error of thinking that any single measure, such as a change in the law, will be a panacea for all drug problems.

When the balance is drawn up in these terms, it is

possible to avoid most of the useless and unproductive argument that has gone on about the drug question and has sometimes tended to over-shadow the earnest and productive discussions which have gone on simultaneously. This approach helps one to keep the question of drug use in the context of the overall pattern of our society and our views toward it.

In general, it is probably fair to say that every benefit resulting from some act of society is purchased at a cost, and the real purpose of the balance we have suggested is to permit people to decide whether, in their opinion, the benefit is worth the price paid. If the question is not put consciously in those terms, there is a tendency for the decision to be made by an unconscious type of balance in which the scales are loaded on the side of the familiar against the unfamiliar. We tend to prefer that to which we are already accustomed. This perhaps explains the tendency of many people, including many law enforcement agencies, to prefer the harms and disadvantages arising from the use of known substances, such as alcohol and barbiturates, to those arising from the use of substances with which we are not yet as familiar, even though no proper quantitative comparison has been made between them.

It may be that after a careful balance of the type which we have suggested, most people will still hold the same views as at present; or it may be that there will be a choice in favor of various legal, social, and educational changes. In either case, if the decision is made by a deliberate effort to reach an informed, dispassionate evaluation, there is a greater chance that it will have the support of a substantial majority and so will permit the government to act with confidence in the name of the whole population. Regardless of the decision which is finally made, the exercise will be well worth while if it enables us to reach such a resolution of the present conflict.

References

REFERENCES: PREFACE

1 Cohen, S. *The Drug Dilemma.* Toronto, 1969. McGraw-Hill.
2 Commission of Inquiry into the Non-Medical Use of Drugs. *Interim Report.* Ottawa, 1970. Queen's Printer for Canada.
3 Goode, E. *Marijuana.* New York, 1969. Atherton Press.
4 Nowlis, H. *Drugs on the College Campus.* Rochester, N.Y., 1967. NASPA Drug Education Project. University of Rochester.
5 Whitaker, R. *Drugs and the Law. The Canadian Scene.* Toronto, 1969. Methuen Publications.

REFERENCES FOR CHAPTER 1

1 Kalant, O.J. *Who Qualifies as a Marijuana Expert?* The Globe and Mail. Toronto, June 17, 1970. Reprinted in: Addictions, Spring, 1971.
2 Ledermann, S. *Can One Reduce Alcoholism without Changing Total Alcohol Consumption in a Population?* Selected Papers, 27th International Congress on Alcohol and Alcoholism. Frankfurt, 1964, vol. 2, p. 1.
3 McGlothlin, W.H., & West, L.J. *The Marihuana Problem: An Overview.* American Journal of Psychiatry *125,* 370, 1968.

4   Smart, R.G., Fejer, D., & White, J. *The Extent of Drug Use in Metropolitan Toronto Schools: A Study of Changes from 1968 to 1970.* Toronto, 1970. Addiction Research Foundation.

REFERENCES FOR CHAPTER 2

1   Abramson, H.A. (ed.) *The Use of LSD in Psychotherapy and Alcoholism.* Indianapolis, 1967. Bobbs-Merrill.
2   Allentuck, S., & Bowman, K.M. *The Psychiatric Aspects of Marihuana Intoxication.* American Journal of Psychiatry *99*, 248, 1942-43.
3   Bradley, P.B., & Key, B.J. *The Effects of Drugs on Arousal Responses Produced by Electrical Stimulation of the Reticular Formation of the Brain.* Electroencephalography and Clinical Neurophysiology *10*, 97, 1958.
4   Brady, J.V. *Emotional Behavior.* In: *Handbook of Physiology.* Section 1: *Neurophysiology.* Vol. III. American Physiological Society, 1960. p. 1553.
5   Bustos, G.O., Kalant, H., Khanna, J.M., & Loth, J. *Pyrazole and Induction of Fatty Liver by a Single Dose of Ethanol.* Science *168*, 1598, 1970.
6   Chance, M.R.A. *Factors Influencing the Toxicity of Sympathomimetic Amines to Solitary Mice.* Journal of Pharmacology and Experimental Therapeutics *89*, 289, 1947.
7   Cohen, S. *The Drug Dilemma.* Toronto, 1969. McGraw-Hill.
8   Commission of Inquiry into the Non-Medical Use of Drugs. *Interim Report.* Ottawa, 1970. Queen's Printer for Canada.
9   Connell, P.H. *Amphetamine Psychosis.* London, 1958. Chapman & Hall.
10 Cox, C., & Smart, R.G. *The Nature and Extent of Speed Use in North America.* Canadian Medical Association Journal *102*, 724, 1970.
11 De Quincy, T. *Confessions of an English Opium-Eater.* London, 1956. Macdonald. (First Published in 1822; revised in 1856).
12 Ellinwood, E.H., Jr. *Amphetamine Psychosis: A Multidimensional Process.* Seminars in Psychiatry *1*, 208, 1969.
13 Essig, C.F. *Addiction to Non-barbiturate Sedatives and Tranquilizing Drugs.* Clinical Pharmacology and Therapeutics *5*, 334, 1964.
14 Garriott, J.C., King, L.J., Forney, R.B., & Hughes, F.W. *Effects of Some Tetrahydrocannabinols on Hexobarbital Sleeping Time and Amphetamine Induced Hyperactivity in Mice.* Life Sciences *6*, 2119, 1967.
15 Gibbins, R.J., Kalant, H., & Le Blanc, A.E. *A Technique for Accurate Measurement of Moderate Degrees of Alcohol Intoxication in Small Animals.* Journal of Pharmacology and Experimental Therapeutics *159*, 236, 1968.

16 Goldberg, L. *Quantitative Studies on Alcohol Tolerance in Man. The Influence of Ethyl Alcohol on Sensory, Motor and Psychological Functions Referred to Blood Alcohol in Normal and Habituated Individuals.* Acta Physiologica Scandinavica 5, Supplement 16, 1943.

17 Goldberg, L. *The Definition of an Intoxicating Beverage.* Quarterly Journal of Studies on Alcohol *16*, 316, 1955.

18 Goode, E. *Marijuana.* New York, 1969. Atherton Press.

19 Goode, E. *Marihuana and the Politics of Reality.* Journal of Health and Social Behavior *10*, 83, 1969.

20 Hartocollis, P. *Drunkenness and Suggestion: An Experiment with Intravenous Alcohol.* Quarterly Journal of Studies on Alcohol *23*, 376, 1962.

21 Hoffer, A., & Osmond, H. *The Hallucinogens.* New York, 1967. Academic Press.

22 Hollister, L.E. *Chemical Psychoses. LSD and Related Drugs.* Springfield, 1968. C.C Thomas.

23 Hollister, L.E., & Gillespie, H.K. *Similarities and Differences Between the Effects of Lysergic Acid Diethylamide and Tetrahydrocannabinol in Man.* In: *Drugs and Youth.* Wittenborn, J.R. *et al.* (eds.) 1969. p 208.

24 Howard-Jones, N. *The Origins of Hypodermic Medication.* Scientific American *224*, No. 1, 96, 1971.

25 Isbell, H., Gorodetzsky, C.W., Jasinski, D., Claussen, U., von Spulak, F., & Korte, F. *Effects of (−) − Δ^9 − Trans-Tetrahydrocannabinol in Man.* Psychopharmacologia *11*, 184, 1967.

26 Isbell, H., & Jasinski, D.R. *A Comparison of LSD-25 with (−) − Δ^9 − Trans-Tetrahydrocannabinol (THC) and Attempted Cross Tolerance Between LSD and THC.* Psychopharmacologia *14*, 115, 1969.

27 Jaffe, J.H. *Narcotic Analgesics.* In: Goodman, L.S., & Gilman, A. *The Pharmacological Basis of Therapeutics.* London & Toronto, 1970. 4th ed. Macmillan. p. 237.

28 James, W. *The Varieties of Religious Experience.* New York, 1902. Longmans.

29 Jarvik, M.E. *Drugs Used in the Treatment of Psychiatric Disorders.* In: Goodman, L.S. & Gilman, A. *The Pharmacological Basis of Therapeutics.* London & Toronto, 1970. 4th ed. Macmillan. p. *151*.

30 Kalant, H. *Effects of Ethanol on the Nervous System.* In: J. Trémolières (ed.) *International Encyclopedia of Pharmacology and Therapeutics.* Section 20, vol. 1. *Alcohols and Derivatives.* Oxford & New York, 1970. Pergamon Press. p. 189.

31 Kalant, H., & Khanna, J.M. *Effects of Chronic Ethanol Intake on Metabolic Pathways.* In: Sardesai, V.M. (ed.) *Biochemical and Clinical Aspects of Alcohol Metabolism.* Springfield, 1969. C.C Thomas. Chapter 7, p. 47.

32 Kalant, O.J. *The Amphetamines. Toxicity and Addiction.* Toronto, 1966. University of Toronto Press.

33 Kalant, O.J. *An Interim Guide to the Cannabis (Marihuana) Literature.* Addiction Research Foundation Bibliographic Series No. 2, 1968.

34 Kalant, O.J. *Ludlow on Cannabis. A Modern Look at a Nineteenth Century Drug Experience.* International Journal of the Addictions *6*, 309, 1971.

35 Keeler, M.H., Reifler, C.B., & Liptzin, M.B. *Spontaneous Recurrence of Marihuana Effect.* American Journal of Psychiatry *125*, 384, 1968.

36 Killam, E.K. *Drug Action on the Brain-stem Reticular Formation.* Pharmacological Reviews *14*, 175, 1962.

37 Klüver, H. *Mescal and Mechanisms of Hallucinations.* Chicago, 1966. University of Chicago Press.

38 LaBarre, W. *The Peyote Cult.* Yale University Publications in Anthropology. No. 19, 1938.

39 Lelbach, W.K. *Liver Cell Necrosis in Rats After Prolonged Ethanol Ingestion Under the Influence of an Alcohol-dehydrogenase Inhibitor.* Experientia *25*, 816, 1969.

40 Lieber, C.S. *Metabolic Derangement Induced by Alcohol.* Annual Review of Medicine *18*, 35, 1967.

41 Lindsley, D.B. *Attention, Consciousness, Sleep and Wakefulness.* In: *Handbook of Physiology.* Secion 1: *Neurophysiology.* Vol. III. American Physiological Society, 1960. p. 1553.

42 Loeb, E.M. *Primitive Intoxicants.* Quarterly Journal of Studies on Alcohol *4*, 387, 1943-44.

43 Lundquist, F. *The Metabolism of Alcohol.* In: Israel, Y. & Mardones, J. (eds.) *Biological Basis of Alcoholism.* New York, 1971 (In Press). Wiley. Chapter 1.

44 Maynert, E.W. *Sedatives and Hypnotics II: Barbiturates.* In: DiPalma, J.R. (ed.) *Drill's Pharmacology in Medicine.* New York, 1965. 3rd ed. McGraw-Hill. p. 201.

45 McGlothlin, W.H. *Cannabis: A Reference.* In: Solomon, D. (ed.) *The Marihuana Papers.* New York, 1966. Bobbs-Merrill. p. 455.

46 Mechoulam, R., Shani, A., Edery, H., & Grunfeld, Y. *Chemical Basis of Hashish Activity.* Science *169*, 611, 1970.

47 Mikuriya, T.H. *Marijuana in Medicine: Past, Present and Future.* California Medicine *110*, 34, 1969.

48 Milman, D.H. *The Role of Marihuana in Patterns of Drug Abuse by Adolescents.* Journal of Pediatrics *74*, 283, 1969.

49 Moe, G.K., & Farah, A.E. *Cardiovascular Drugs. Digitalis and Allied Cardiac Glycosides.* In: Goodman, L.S. & Gilman, A. *The Pharmacological Basis of Therapeutics.* London & Toronto, 1970. 4th ed. Macmillan. p. 677.

50 Murphy, H.B.M. *The Cannabis Habit. A Review of Recent Psychiatric Literature.* Bulletin on Narcotics *15,* 15, 1963.

51 Newman, H.W. *Alcohol Injected Intravenously. Some Psychological and Psychopathological Effects in Man.* American Journal of Psychiatry *91,* 1343, 1935.

52 Olds, J. *Self-stimulation of the Brain. Its Use to Study Local Effects of Hunger, Sex and Drugs.* Science *127,* 315, 1958.

53 Perna, D. *Psychotogenic Effect of Marihuana.* Journal of the American Medical Association *209,* 1085, 1969.

54 Polacsek, E. *Interaction of Alcohol and Other Drugs. An Annotated Bibliography.* Addiction Research Foundation Bibliographic Series No. 3, 1970.

55 Popham, R.E. (ed.) *Alcohol and Alcoholism.* Toronto, 1970. University of Toronto Press.

56 Ritchie, J.M. *The Aliphatic Alcohols.* In: Goodman, L.S. & Gilman, A. *The Pharmacological Basis of Therapeutics.* London & Toronto, 1970. 4th ed. Macmillan. p. 145.

57 Ritchie, J.M. *Central Nervous Stimulants. II. Xanthines. Caffeine, Theophylline, and Theobromine.* In: Goodman, L.S. & Gilman, A. *The Pharmacological Basis of Therapeutics.* London & Toronto, 1970. 4th Ed. Macmillan. p. 358.

58 Rodin, E.A., Domino, E.F., & Porzak, J.P. *The Marihuana-Induced "Social High".* Journal of the American Medical Association *213,* 1300, 1970.

59 Roper, P. *Drug Addiction, Psychotic Illness and Brain Self-Stimulation.* Canadian Medical Association Journal *95,* 1080, 1966.

60 Sharpless, S.K. *Hypnotics and Sedatives.* In: Goodman, L.S. & Gilman, A. *The Pharmacological Basis of Therapeutics.* London & Toronto, 1970. 4th ed. Macmillan. p. 98.

61 Slotkin, J.S. *The Peyote Religion.* New York, 1956. Free Press of Glencoe.

62 Smart, R.G., & Bateman, K. *Unfavorable Reactions to LSD.* Canadian Medical Association Journal *97,* 1214, 1967.

63 Smart, R.G., Storm, T., Baker, E.F.W., & Solursh, L. *Lysergic Acid Diethylamide (LSD) in the Treatment of Alcoholism.* Toronto, 1967. University of Toronto Press.

64 Smith, D.E., & Mehl, C. *An Analysis of Marijuana Toxicity.* Clinical Toxicology *3,* 101, 1970.

65 Takala, M., Pihkanen, T.A., & Markkanen, T. *The Effects of Distilled and Brewed Beverages: A Physiological, Neurological and Psychological Study.* Finnish Foundation of Alcohol Studies. vol. 4, Helsinki, 1957.

66 Talbott, J.A., & Teague, J.W. *Marihuana Psychosis. Acute Toxic Psychosis Associated with the Use of Cannabis Derivatives.* Journal of the American Medical Association *210,* 299, 1969.

67 U.N. Drug Supervisory Body. *Estimated World Requirements of Narcotic Drugs in 1966.* Bulletin on Narcotics *18,* 50, 1966.

68 Unwin, J.R. *Non-Medical Use of Drugs. With Particular Reference to Youth.* Canadian Medical Association Journal *101*, 804, 1969.

69 Valle, J.R. *Pharmacological Approaches to the Study of the Cannabis Problem.* International Journal of the Addictions *4*, 623, 1969.

70 Victor, M. *Alcohol and Nutritional Diseases of the Nervous System.* Journal of the American Medical Association *167*, 65, 1958.

71 Volle, R.L., & Koelle, G.B. *Ganglionic Stimulating and Blocking Agents.* In: Goodman, L.S. & Gilman, A. *The Pharmacological Basis of Therapeutics.* London & Toronto, 1970. 4th ed. Macmillan. p. 588.

72 Walton, R.P. *Marihuana – America's New Drug Problem.* New York, 1938. Lippincott.

73 Wei, P., Hamilton, J.R., & LeBlanc, A.E. *Intravenous Feeding of Infants and Children by Peripheral Vein. Clinical and Metabolic Study of 15 Cases.* Paper Presented at the Annual Meeting of the Royal College of Physicians and Surgeons of Canada, Ottawa, January, 1971.

74 Weil, A.T., Zinberg, N.E., & Nelsen, J.M. *Clinical and Psychological Effects of Marihuana in Man.* Science *162*, 1234, 1968.

75 Weiss, B., & Laties, V.G. *Enhancement of Human Performance by Caffeine and the Amphetamines.* Pharmacological Reviews *14*, 1, 1962.

76 Williams, E.G., Himmelsbach, C.K., Wikler, A., Ruble, D.C., & Lloyd, B.J. *Studies on Marihuana and Pyrahexyl Compound.* Public Health Reports *61*, 1059, 1946.

REFERENCES FOR CHAPTER 3

1 Aldrich, C.K. *The Effect of a Synthetic Marihuana-like Compound on Musical Talent as Measured by the Seashore Test.* Public Health Reports *59*, 431, 1944.

2 Anonymous. *Potted Dreams.* British Medical Journal *i*, 133, 1969.

3 Bacon, S. *Alcohol and Congolese Society.* In: Pittman, D.J. & Snyder, C.R. (eds.) *Society, Culture and Drinking Patterns.* New York, 1962. Wiley.

4 Bales, R.F. *Cultural Differences in Rates of Alcoholism.* Quarterly Journal of Studies on Alcohol *6*, 480, 1946.

5 Baudelaire, C. *Les Paradis Artificiels.* Paris, 1964. Gallimard & Librairie Générale Française. (First Published in 1860). English translation in: Symons, A. (tr.) *Baudelaire – Prose and Poetry.* New York, 1926. Albert & Charles Boni.

6 Benabud, A. *Psycho-pathological Aspects of the Cannabis Situation in Morocco: Statistical Data for 1956*. Bulletin on Narcotics *9*, 1, 1957.

7 Blumer, H., Sutter, A., Ahmed, S., & Smith, R. *The World of Youthful Drug Use*. ADD Centre Project Final Report. Berkeley, California, 1967. School of Criminology, University of California. Mimeo.

8 Brésard, M. *Présentation d'une Enquête sur la Consommation des Boissons en France*. Bulletin de l'Institut National d'Hygiène *13*, 267, 1958.

9 Bruun, K. *Significance of Role and Norms in the Small Group for Individual Behavioral Changes While Drinking*. Quarterly Journal of Studies on Alcohol *20*, 53, 1959.

10. Cahalan, D., Cisin, I., & Crossley, H. *American Drinking Practices. A National Survey of Behavior and Attitudes Related to Alcoholic Beverages*. Report No. 3, Social Research Group. The George Washington University. June, 1967.

11 Chopra, R.N., &Chopra, G.S. *The Present Position of Hemp-Drug Addiction in India*. Indian Journal of Medical Research (Supplementary Series) Memoir No. 31. Calcutta, 1939.

12 Commission of Inquiry into the Non-Medical Use of Drugs. *Interim Report*. Ottawa, 1970. Queen's Printer for Canada.

13 Cooperstock, R., & Sims, M. *Mood-Modifying Drugs Prescribed in a Canadian City: Hidden Problems*. American Journal of Public Health (In Press). See also: Addiction Research Foundation Substudy 1 – 31 & 29 – 69.

14 Doll, R., & Hill, A.B. *Mortality in Relation to Smoking: Ten Years' Observation of British Doctors*. British Medical Journal *i*, 1399, 1964.

15 Ebin, D. (ed.) *The Drug Experience*. New York, 1961. The Orion Press.

16 Efron, D.H., Holstedt, B., & Kline, N.S. (eds.) *Ethnopharmacologic Search for Psychoactive Drugs*. Washington, 1967. U.S. Department of Health, Education and Welfare. Public Health Service Publications No. 1645.

17 Encel, S., & Kotowicz K. *Heavy Drinking and Alcoholism*. Medical Journal of Australia *i*, 607, 1970.

18 Gadourek, I. *Riskante Gewoonten*. Groningen, Holland, 1963. Wolters.

19 Gautier, T. *Le Club des Hachichins*. Paris, 1964. Gallimard & Librairie Générale Française. (First Published in 1846). English translation in: Solomon, D. (ed.) *The Marihuana Papers*. Indianapolis, 1966. Bobbs-Merrill.

20 Goode, E. *The Marijuana Smokers*. New York & London, 1970. Basic Books.

21 Harman, W.W., McKim, R.H., Mogar, R.E., *et al. Psychedelic Agents in Creative Problem Solving: A Pilot Study.* Psychological Reports *19,* 211, 1966.

22 Hartmann, R. *The Artificial Paradises* (Film). Reported in: Time, December 5, 1969.

23 Huxley, A. *The Doors of Perception.* Harmondsworth, Middlesex, 1963. (First Published by Chatto and Windus, 1954).

24 Hyde, M.O. *Mind Drugs.* New York, 1968. McGraw-Hill.

25 Kalant, O.J. *The Amphetamines. Toxicity and Addiction.* Toronto, 1966. University of Toronto Press.

26 Kalant, O.J. *Moreau, Hashish and Hallucinations.* International Journal of the Addictions 6, 553, 1971.

27 Kalant, O.J. *Report of the Indian Hemp Drugs Commission – 1893-1894. A Critical Review.* International Journal of the Addictions 7, 77, 1972.

28 Kramer, J.C., Fischman, V.S., & Littlefield, D.C. *Amphetamine Abuse.* Journal of the American Medical Association *201,* 305, 1967.

29 LaBarre, W. *The Peyote Cult.* Yale University Publications in Anthropology. No. 19, 1938.

30 Malcolm, A.I. *The Pursuit of Intoxication.* Toronto, 1971. Addiction Research Foundation.

31 Manheimer, D.I., Mellinger, G.D., & Balter, M.B. *Marijuana Use Among Urban Adults.* Science *166,* 1544, 1969.

32 *Memorandum on Drug Abuse in Sweden.* Presented to the United Nations Narcotics Commission Meeting, Geneva, March, 1968.

33 Moreau (de Tours), J. *Du Hachich et de l'Aliénation Mentale.* Paris, 1945. Masson.

34 Oki, G., & Sisson, B.V. *Interim Report of the Marihuana Study Project.* Addiction Research Foundation Substudy 1 – 16 & 34 – 69.

35 Popham, R.E. *The Jellinek Alcoholism Estimation Formula and its Application to Canadian Data.* Quarterly Journal of Studies on Alcohol *17,* 559, 1956.

36 Popham, R.E. *The Urban Tavern; Some Preliminary Remarks.* Addictions *9,* 16, 1962.

37 Popham, R.E., & Schmidt, W. *Statistics of Alcohol Use and Alcoholism in Canada. 1871-1956.* Toronto, 1958. University of Toronto Press.

38 Popham, R.E. & Yawney, C. *The Symbolism of Drinking: A Culture-historical Approach by E.M. Jellinek.* Addiction Research Foundation Substudy 3 – 2 & Y – 65.

39 Prove. W. *Summary of an Investigation of Selected Drinking Habits of Students at the University of Gent.* Translated by de Lint, J. & Schmidt, W. Addiction Research Foundation Substudy 8 – 10 & 4 – 65.

40 *Report of the Indian Hemp Drugs Commission—1893-1894.* Simla, 1894. Government Printing Office. Reprinted: Kaplan, J. (ed.) *Marijuana. Report of the Indian Hemp Drugs Commission. 1893-1894.* Silver Spring, Maryland, 1969. Thos. Jefferson.

41 *Report of the Inter-Departmental Committee on the Abuse of Dagga.* Union of South Africa. Pretoria, 1952. The Government Printer.

42 Salber, E.J., & McMahon, B. *Cigarette Smoking among High School Students as Related to Social Class and Parental Smoking Habits.* American Journal of Public Health *51*, 1780, 1961.

43 Seashore, R.H., & Ivy, A.C. *Effects of Analeptic Drugs in Relieving Fatigue.* Psychological Monographs *67*, 1, 1952.

44 Seeley, J.R. *Death by Liver Cirrhosis and the Price of Beverage Alcohol.* Canadian Medical Association Journal *83*,1361, 1960.

45 Slotkin, J.S. *The Peyote Religion.* New York, 1956. Free Press of Glencoe.

46 Smart, R.G., & Fejer, D. *Drug Use among Adolescents and Their Parents: Closing the Generation Gap in Mood Modification.* Addiction Research Foundation Substudy 3 – 7 & Jo – 70.

47 Smart, R.G., Fejer, D., & White, J. *The Extent of Drug Use in Metropolitan Toronto Schools: A Study of Changes from 1968 to 1970.* Toronto, 1970. Addiction Research Foundation.

48 Smart, R.G., & Jackson, D. *The Yorkville Subculture: A Study of the Life Styles and Interactions of Hippies and Non-hippies.* Addiction Research Foundation Substudy 1 – 7 & Ja – 69.

49 Soueif, M.I. *Hashish Consumption in Egypt with Special Reference to Psychosocial Aspects.* Bulletin on Narcotics *19*, 1, 1967.

50 Williams, E.G., Himmelsbach, C.K., Wikler, A., Ruble, D.C., & Lloyd, B.J. *Studies on Marihuana and Pyrahexyl Compound.* Public Health Reports *61*, 1059, 1946.

51 Winfield, R. *The Use of Benzedrine to Overcome Fatigue on Operational Flights in Bomber Command.* Great Britain (no date). Flight Personnel Research Committee. Report No. 433.

52 Zapata-Ortiz, V. *The Chewing of Coca Leaves in Perú.* International Journal of the Addictions *5*, 287, 1970.

53 Zegans, L.S., Pollard, J.C., & Brown, D. *The Effects of LSD-25 on Creativity and Tolerance to Regression.* Archives of General Psychiatry *16*, 740, 1967.

REFERENCES FOR CHAPTER 4

1 Becker, H.S. *Becoming a Marihuana User.* American Journal of Sociology *59*, 235, 1958.

2 Beckett, A.H., & Rowland, M. *Urinary Excretion of Amphetamine in Man.* Journal of Pharmacy and Pharmacology *17*, 628, 1965.

3 Benabud, A. *Psycho-pathological Aspects of the Cannabis Situation in Morocco: Statistical Data for 1956.* Bulletin on Narcotics *9*, 1, 1957.

4 Bischof, H.L. *Zur Pathogenese des Alkoholdelirs.* Nervenarzt *40*, 318, 1969.

5 Black, M.B., Woods, J.H., & Domino, E.F. *Some Effects of (−) − △⁹ − Trans-Tetrahydrocannabinol and Other Cannabis Derivatives on Schedule-controlled Behavior.* Pharmacologist *12*, 258, 1970.

6 Cherubin, G.E. *The Medical Sequelae of Narcotic Addiction.* Annals of Internal Medicine *67*, 23, 1967.

7 Chopra, R.N., & Chopra, G.S. *The Present Position of Hempdrug Addiction in India.* Indian Journal of Medical Research [Supplementary Series] Memoir No. 31. Calcutta, 1939.

8 Cholden, L.S., Kurland, A., & Savage, C. *Clinical Reactions and Tolerance to LSD in Chronic Schizophrenia.* Journal of Nervous and Mental Disease *122*, 211, 1955.

9 Connell, P.H. *Amphetamine Psychosis.* London, 1958. Chapman & Hall.

10 Conney, A.H. *Pharmacological Implications of Microsomal Enzyme Induction.* Pharmacological Reviews *19*, 317, 1967.

11 Cordeiro De Farias, R. *Use of Maconha (Cannabis sativa L.) in Brazil.* Bulletin on Narcotics *7*, 5, 1955.

12 Cox, C., & Smart, R.G. *The Nature and Extent of Speed Use in North America.* Canadian Medical Association Journal *102*, 724, 1970.

13 Dewey, W.L., Harris, L.S., Howes, J.F., & Kennedy, J.S. *Pharmacological Effects of Some Active Constitutents of Marihuana.* Pharmacologist *11*, 272, 1969.

14 Elliot, H.W., Tolbert, B.M., Adler, T.K., & Anderson, H.H. *Excretion of Carbon-14 by Man After Administration of Morphine-N-methyl-C¹⁴.* Proceedings of the Society for Experimental Biology and Medicine *85*, 77, 1954.

15 Essig, C.F. *Addiction to Non-barbiturate Sedatives and Tranquilizing Drugs.* Clinical Pharmacology and Therapeutics *5*, 334, 1964.

16 Essig, C.F. *Addiction to Barbiturate and Non-barbiturate Sedative Drugs.* In: Wikler, A. (ed.) *The Addictive States.* Baltimore, 1968. Williams & Wilkins.

16a. Fehr, K. O'B., & Kalant, H. *Analysis of Cannabis Smoke Obtained under Different Combustion Conditions.* Canadian Journal of Physiology and Pharmacology *50*, July 1972.

17 Finnegan, J.K., Larson, P.S., & Haag, H.B. *The Role of Nicotine*

in the Cigarette Habit. Science *102,* 94, 1945.

18 Fränkel, S. *Chemie und Pharmakologie des Haschisch.* Archiv für experimentelle Pathologie und Pharmakologie *49,* 266, 1903.

19 Freedman, D.X. *The Psychopharmacology of Hallucinogenic Agents.* Annual Review of Medicine *20,* 409, 1969.

20 Garakushansky, G., Neu, R.L., & Gardner, L.I. *Lysergide and Cannabis as Possible Teratogens in Man.* Lancet *i,* 150, 1969.

21 Gibbins, R.J. Personal communication.

22 Gill, E.W., Paton, W.D.M., & Pertwee, R.G. *Preliminary Experiments on the Chemistry and Pharmacology of Cannabis.* Nature *228,* 134, 1970.

23 Glatt, M.M. *The Abuse of Barbiturates in the United Kingdom.* Bulletin on Narcotics *14,* 19, 1962.

24 Hecht, F., Beals, R.K., Lees, M.H. & Roberts, P. *Lysergic-Acid-Diethylamide and Cannabis as Possible Teratogens in Man.* Lancet *ii,* 1087, 1968.

25 Henderson, A.H., & Pugsley, D.J. *Collapse After Intravenous Use of Hashish.* British Medical Journal *iii,* 229, 1968.

26 Isbell, H., & Fraser, H.F. *Addiction to Analgesics and Barbiturates.* Pharmacological Reviews *2,* 355, 1950.

27 Isbell, H., & Jasinski, D.R. *A Comparison of LSD-25 with (−) − Δ^9 −Trans-Tetrahydrocannabinol (THC) and Attempted Cross Tolerance Between LSD and THC.* Psychopharmacologia *14,* 115, 1969.

28 Jaffe, J.H. *Drug Addiction and Drug Abuse.* In: Goodman, L.S. & Gilman, A. (eds.) *The Pharmacological Basis of Therapeutics.* London & Toronto, 1970. 4th ed. Macmillan. Chapter 16.

29 Kalant, O.J. *The Amphetamines. Toxicity and Addiction.* Toronto, 1966. University of Toronto Press.

30 Kalant, O.J. *An Interim Guide to the Cannabis (Marihuana) Literature.* Addiction Research Foundation Bibliographic Series No. 2, 1968.

31 Kalant, O.J. *Ludlow on Cannabis. A Modern Look at a Nineteenth Century Drug Experience.* International Journal of the Addictions 6, 309, 1971.

32 Kalant, O.J. *Report of the Indian Hemp Drugs Commission − 1893-1894. A Critical Review.* International Journal of the Addictions *7,* 77, 1972.

33 Kaplan, J. *Marijuana. Report of the Indian Hemp Drugs Commission. 1893-1894.* Silver Spring, Maryland, 1969. Thos. Jefferson.

34 Khanna, J.M., Kalant, H., & Bustos, G. *Effects of Chronic Intake of Ethanol on Rate of Ethanol Metabolism. II. Influence of Sex and of Schedule of Ethanol Administration.* Canadian Journal of Physiology and Pharmacology *45,* 777, 1967.

35 King, A.B., & Cowen, D.L. *Effect of Intravenous Injection of Marihuana.* Journal of the American Medical Association *210,* 724, 1969.

36. Knapp, P.H., Bliss, C.M., & Wells, H. *Addictive Aspects in Heavy Cigarette Smoking.* American Journal of Psychiatry *119*, 966, 1963.

37 Kramer, J.C. *Introduction to Amphetamine Abuse.* Journal of Psychedelic Drugs *2*, 1, 1969.

38 Kramer, J.C., Fischman, V.S. & Littlefield, D.C. *Amphetamine Abuse.* Journal of the American Medical Association *201*, 305, 1967.

39 Kreuger, H., Eddy, N., & Sumwalt, M. *The Pharmacology of the Opium Alkaloids: Part 1 & 2.* Public Health Reports, Supplement No. 165, 1943.

40 Le Blanc, A.E., Kalant, H., & Kalant, O.J. *The Psychopharmacology of Amphetamine Dependence.* Applied Therapeutics *12*, 30, 1970.

41 Leevy, C.M., Tamburro, C., & Smith, F. *Alcoholism, Drug Addiction and Nutrition.* Medical Clinics of North America *54*, 1567, 1970.

42 Lelbach, W.K. *Liver Cell Necrosis in Rats after Prolonged Ethanol Ingestion under the Influence of an Alcohol-dehydrogenase Inhibitor.* Experientia *25*, 816, 1969.

43 Lemberger, L., Silberstein, S.D., Axelrod, J., & Kopin, I.J. *Marihuana: Studies on the Disposition and Metabolism of Delta-9-Tetrahydrocannabinol in Man.* Science *170*, 1320, 1970.

44 Louria, D.B., Hensle, R., & Rose, J. *The Major Medical Complications of Heroin Addiction.* Annals of Internal Medicine *67*, 1, 1967.

45 Manheimer, D.I., Mellinger, G.D., & Balter, M.B. *Marijuana Use Among Urban Adults.* Science *166*, 1544, 1969.

46 Marshman, J.A., & Gibbins, R.J. *A Note on the Composition of Illicit Drugs.* Ontario Medical Review p. 1, September, 1970.

47 McMillan, D.E., Harris, L.S., Frankenheim, J.M., & Kennedy, J.S. *1-$\triangle^9$-trans-Tetrahydrocannabinol in Pigeons: Tolerance to the Behavioral Effects.* Science *169*, 501, 1970.

48 McWilliams, P. *The Formidable Cost of Enforcing Marihuana Laws.* The Globe and Mail. Toronto, December 31, 1970.

49 Moreton, J.E., & Davis, W.M. *Effects of $\triangle-9-$Tetrahydrocannabinol on Locomotor Activity and on Phases of Sleep.* Pharmacologist *12*, 258, 1970.

50 Neu, R.L., Powers, H.O., King, S., & Gardner, L.I. $\triangle^8-$ and $\triangle^9$-*Tetrahydrocannabinol: Effects on Cultured Human Leucocytes.* Journal of Clinical Pharmacology *10*, 228, 1970.

51 Persaud, T.V.N., & Ellington, A.C. *The Effects of Cannabis sativa L. (Ganja) on Developing Rat Embryos – Preliminary Observations.* West Indian Medical Journal *17*, 232, 1968.

52 Ploscowe, M. *Some Basic Problems in Drug Addiction and Suggestions for Research.* In: Joint Committee of the American Bar Association and the American Medical Association on

Narcotic Drugs, *Drug Addiction: Crime or Disease?*Blooming-
ton, 1961. Indiana University Press.

53 Popham. R.E. (ed.) *Alcohol and Alcoholism.* Toronto, 1970.
University of Toronto Press.

54 Servico Nacional de Educação Sanitaria. *Maconha (Coletanea de
Trabalhos Brasileiros).* Rio de Janeiro, 1958. Ministerio de
Saude.

55 Silva, M.T.A., Carlini, E.A., Claussen, U., & Korte, F. *Lack of
Cross-Tolerance in Rats Among (−)△⁹-Trans-Tetrahydrocan-
nabinol (△⁹-THC), Cannabis Extract, Mescaline and Lysergic
Acid Diethylamide (LSD-25).* Psychopharmacologia *13,* 332,
1969.

56 Smart, R.G., & Bateman, K. *The Chromosomal and Teratogenic
Effects of Lysergic Acid Diethylamide.* Canadian Medical Association Journal *99,* 805, 1968.

57 Smith, D.E., & Mehl, C. *An Analysis of Marijuana Toxicity.*
Clinical Toxicology *3,* 101, 1970.

58 Tormey, J., & Lasagna, L. *Relation of Thyroid Function to
Acute and Chronic Effects of Amphetamine in the Rat.* Journal
of Pharmacology and Experimental Therapeutics *128,* 201,
1960.

59 Victor, M. *Alcohol and Nutritional Diseases of the Nervous
System.* Journal of the American Medical Association *167,* 65,
1958.

60 Victor, M. *The Treatment of Alcoholism.* In: J. Trémolières (ed.)
International Encyclopedia of Pharmacology and Therapeutics.
Section 20, Vol. 1. *Alcohols and Derivatives.* Oxford & New
York, 1970. Pergamon Press.

61 Weil, A.T., Zinberg, N.E., & Nelsen, J.M. *Clinical and Psychological Effects of Marihuana in Man.* Science *162,* 1234, 1968.

62 Wendt, V.E., Puro, H.E., Shapiro, J., Mathews, W., & Wolf, P.L.
Angiothrombotic Pulmonary Hypertension in Addicts. Journal
of the American Medical Association *188,* 755, 1964.

63 Williams, E.G., Himmelsbach, C.K., Wikler, A., Ruble, D.C., &
Lloyd, B.J. *Studies on Marihuana and Pyrahexyl Compound.*
Public Health Reports *61,* 1059, 1946.

REFERENCES CHAPTER 5

1 Blacker, K.H., Jones, R.T., Stone, G.C., & Pfefferbaum, D.
Chronic Users of LSD: The "Acidheads". American Journal of
Psychiatry *125,* 341, 1968.

2 Cahalan, D. *Problem Drinkers.* San Francisco, 1970. Jossey-Bass.

3 Cohen, S. *The Drug Dilemma.* Toronto, 1969. McGraw-Hill.
More details are provided in a paper entitled, *"LSD and Organic
Brain Impairment",* by S. Cohen and A.E. Edwards, read to the

Section on Nervous and Mental Diseases, American Medical Association, San Francisco, June 18, 1968.

4 Colbach, E.M., & Crowe, R.R. *Marihuana-associated Psychosis in Vietnam.* Military Medicine *135,* 571, 1970.

5 Fränkel, S. *Chemie und Pharmakologie des Haschisch.* Archiv für experimentelle Pathologie und Pharmakologie *49, 266, 1903.*

6 Isbell, H., & Fraser, H.F. *Addiction to Analgesics and Barbiturates.* Pharmacological Reviews *2,* 355, 1950.

7 Keup, W. *Psychotic Symptoms Due to Cannabis Abuse.* Diseases of the Nervous System *31,* 119, 1970.

8 Krystal, H., & Raskin, H.A., *Drug Dependence. Aspects of Ego Function.* Detroit, 1970. Wayne State University Press.

9 Le Blanc, A.E., Kalant, H., & Kalant, O.J. *The Psychopharmacology of Amphetamine Dependence.* Applied Therapeutics *12,* 30, 1970.

10 Malcolm, A.I. *The Pursuit of Intoxication.* Toronto, 1971. Addiction Research Foundation.

11 McGlothlin, W.H., & West, L.J. *The Marihuana Problem: An Overview.* American Journal of Psychiatry *125,* 370, 1968.

12 Nielsen, J.M. *Neurology of Alcoholism.* In: Thompson, G.N.P. (ed.) *Alcoholism.* Springfield, 1956. C.C Thomas.

13 Potondi, A., Dömötör, E., & Orvecz, B. *Ueber die Spontanverletzungen Betrunkener.* Acta Chirurgica Academiae Scientiarum Hungaricae *8,* 337, 1967.

14 Royal Commission on Opium. *Final Report of the Royal Commision on Opium.* London, 1895. H.M.S.O.

15 Russell, R.W. *Behavioral Effects of Psychoactive Drugs.* In: Kalant, H. & Hawkins, R.D. (eds.) *Experimental Approaches to the Study of Drug Dependence.* Toronto, 1969. University of Toronto Press.

16 Schmidt, W., & de Lint, J. *Causes of Death of Alcoholics.* Quarterly Journal of Studies on Alcohol. (In press).

17 Schmidt, W., & Smart, R.G. *Alcoholics, Drinking and Traffic Accidents.* Quarterly Journal of Studies on Alcohol *20,* 631, 1959.

18 Solursh, L.P. Personal communication.

19 Sundby, P. *Alcoholism and Mortality.* New Brunswick, N.J. 1967. Rutgers Center on Alcohol Studies.

20 Unwin, J.R. *Non-medical Use of Drugs. With Particular Reference to Youth.* Canadian Medical Association Journal *101,* 804, 1969.

21 Weil, A.T., Zinberg, N.E., & Nelsen, J.M. *Clinical and Psychological Effects of Marihuana in Man.* Science *162,* 1234, 1968.

22 World Health Organization Expert Committee on Addiction-producing Drugs. *Definition of Habit-forming Drugs.* W.H.O. Technical Report Series No. 116, 9, 1957.

23 World Health Organization Expert Committee on Addiction-producing Drugs. *Terminology in Regard to Drug Abuse.* W.H.O. Technical Report Series No. 273, 9, 1964.

REFERENCES CHAPTER 6

1 Ball, J.C., Chambers, C.D., & Ball, M.J. *The Association of Marihuana Smoking with Opiate Addiction in the United States.* Journal of Criminal Law, Criminology and Police Science *59,* 171, 1968.
2 Bateman, K., & Smart, R.G. *Accidental Death During an LSD Reaction: The Importance of Convulsions.* Addiction Research Foundation Substudy 2 – Ba & 7 – 67.
3 Blumer, H., Sutter, A., Ahmed, S., & Smith, R. *The World of Youthful Drug Use.* ADD Center Project Final Report. Berkeley, California, 1967. School of Criminology, University of California. Mimeo.
4 Bromberg, W., & Rodgers, T.C. *Marihuana and Aggressive Crime.* American Journal of Psychiatry *102,* 835, 1945-46.
5 Chopra, R.N., Chopra, G.S., & Chopra, I.C. *Cannabis Sativa in Relation to Mental Diseases and Crime in India.* Indian Journal of Medical Research *30,* 155, 1942.
6 Colbach, E.M., & Crowe, R.R. *Marihuana Associated Psychosis in Vietnam.* Military Medicine *135,* 571, 1970.
7 Commission of Inquiry into the Non-Medical Use of Drugs. *Interim Report.* Ottawa, 1970. Queen's Printer for Canada.
8 Cox, C., & Smart, R.G. *The Nature and Extent of Speed Use in North America.* Canadian Medical Association Journal *102,* 724, 1970.
9 Crancer, A., Jr., Dille, J.M., Delay, J.C., Wallace, J.E., & Haykin, M.D. *Comparison of the Effects of Marihuana and Alcohol on Simulated Driving Performance.* Science *164,* 851, 1969.
10 de Lint, J. Personal communication.
11 Gomila, F.R., & Gomila Lambou, M.C. *Present Status of the Marihuana Vice in the United States.* In: Walton, R.P. *Marihuana – America's New Drug Problem.* Philadelphia, 1938. Lippincott.
12 Hawks, D. *The Dimension of Drug Dependence in the United Kingdom.* Paper Presented to the International Institute on the Prevention and Treatment of Drug Dependence. Lausanne, 1970.
13 Kalant, H. *Marihuana and Simulated Driving.* Science *166,* 640, 1969.
14 Kalant, O.J. *The Amphetamines. Toxicity and Addiction.* Toronto, 1966. University of Toronto Press.
15 Kalant, O.J. *Report of the Indian Hemp Drugs Commission – 1893-1894. A Critical Review.* International Journal of the Addictions 7, 77, 1972.

16 Kibrick, E., & Smart, R.G. *Psychotropic Drug Use and Driving Risk: A Review and Analysis.* Journal of Safety Research *2*, 73, 1970.

17 Lindesmith, A.R. *Opiate Addiction.* Evanston, 1947. Principia.

18 Malcolm, A.I. *Solvent-sniffing and Its Effects.* Addictions *15*, 12, 1968.

19 Manno, J.E., Kiplinger, G.F., Haine, S.E., Bennett, I.F., & Forney, R.B. *Comparative Effects of Smoking Marihuana or Placebo on Human Motor and Mental Performance.* Clinical Pharmacology and Therapeutics *11*, 808, 1970.

20 McGlothlin, W.H., Arnold, D.O., & Rowan, P.K. *Marijuana Use Among Adults.* Psychiatry *33*, 433, 1970.

21 Mechoulam, R. Personal communication.

22 Mohamed, R.A. Personal communication.

23 Munch, J.C. *Marihuana and Crime.* Bulletin on Narcotics *18*, 15, 1966.

24 Murphy, E.F. *The Black Candle.* Toronto, 1922. Allen.

25 Poirier, J. *Les Problèmes de la Consommation du Chanvre Indien au Madagascar.* Lectures Presented at the International Congress on Drug Dependence, Quebec City, 1968. Quebec City: OPTAT 1969. Chapter B-6.

26 Polacsek, E. *Interaction of Alcohol and Other Drugs.* Addiction Research Foundation Bibliographic Series No. 3, 1970.

27 *Report of the Indian Hemp Drugs Commission – 1893-1894.* Simla, 1894. Government Printing Office. Reprinted: Kaplan, J. (ed.) *Marihuana. Report of the Indian Hemp Drugs Commission – 1893-1894.* Silver Spring, Maryland, 1969. Thos. Jefferson.

28 *Report of the Inter-Departmental Committee on the Abuse of Dagga.* Union of South Africa. Pretoria, 1952. The Government Printer.

29 Schmidt, W., Smart, R.G., & Popham, R.E. *The Role of Alcoholism in Motor Vehicle Accidents.* Traffic Safety (Research Review) *6*, 1, 1962.

30 Selzer, M.L., Rogers, J.E., & Kern, S. *Fatal Accidents: The Role of Psychopathology, Social Stress and Acute Disturbance.* American Journal of Psychiatry *124*, 1028, 1968.

31 Smith, D.E., & Mehl, C. *An Analysis of Marijuana Toxicity.* Clinical Toxicology *3*, 101, 1970.

32 Soueif, M.I. *Hashish Consumption in Egypt with Special Reference to Psychosocial Aspects.* Bulletin on Narcotics *19*, 1, 1967.

33 Talbott, J.A., & Teague, J.W. *Marihuana Psychosis. Acute Toxic Psychosis Associated with the Use of Cannabis Derivatives.* Journal of the American Medical Association *210*, 299, 1969.

34 Trice, H.M., & Belasco, J.A. *Job Absenteeism and Drinking Behavior.* Management Personnel Quarterly *6*, 526, 1968.

35 United States Public Health Service Report No. 1043, 1964. *Alcohol and Traffic Safety.*

36 World Health Organization Expert Committee on Addiction-producing Drugs. *Definition of Habit-forming Drugs.* W.H.O. Technical Report Series No. 116, 9, 1957.

REFERENCES CHAPTER 7

1 *Appendices to the Nineteenth Annual Report (1969) of the Alcoholism and Drug Addiction Research Foundation.* Toronto, 1970.

2 Benabud, A. *Psycho-pathological Aspects of the Cannabis Situation in Morocco: Statistical Data for 1956.* Bulletin on Narcotics 9, 1, 1957.

3 Bruun, K., Koura, E., Popham, R.E., & Seeley, J.R. *Liver Cirrhosis Mortality as a Means to Measure the Prevalence of Alcoholism.* Finnish Foundation for Alcohol Studies. Helsinki, 1960.

4 Chopra, R.N., & Chopra, I.C. *Drug Addiction with Special Reference to India.* New Delhi, 1965. Council of Scientific and Industrial Research.

5 Commission of Inquiry into the Non-Medical Use of Drugs. *Interim Report.* Ottawa, 1970. Queen's Printer for Canada.

6 de Lint, J., & Schmidt, W. *The Distribution of Alcohol Consumption in Ontario.* Quarterly Journal of Studies on Alcohol 29, 968, 1968.

7 Devenyi, P., & Wilson, M. *Abuse of Barbiturates in an Alcoholic Population.* Canadian Medical Association Journal 104, 219, 1971.

8 *Gallup Poll of Canada.* Toronto Daily Star, April 8, 1970.

9 Goode, E. *The Marijuana Smokers.* New York & London, 1970. Basic Books.

10 Jollife, N., & Jellinek, E.M. *Cirrhosis of the Liver.* In: *Effects of Alcohol on the Individual.* Jellinek, E.M. (ed.) New Haven, 1942. Yale University Press. vol. I, p. 273.

11 Kalant, O.J. *Report of the Indian Hemp Drugs Commission – 1893-1894. A Critical Review.* International Journal of the Addictions 7, 77, 1972.

12 Ledermann, S. *Alcool – Alcoolisme – Alcoolisation. Données Scientifiques de Caractère Physiologique et Social.* Institut National d'Etudes Démographiques, Travaux et Documents, Cahier No. 29. France, 1956. Presses Universitaires.

13 Ledermann, S. *Can One Reduce Alcoholism without Changing Total Alcohol Consumption in a Population?* Selected Papers, 27th International Congress on Alcohol and Alcoholism. Frankfurt, 1964. vol. 2.

14 Lelbach, W.K. *Leberschaeden bei chronischem Alkoholismus.* Acta Hepato-Splenologica 14, 9, 1967.

15 Manheimer, D.I., Mellinger, G.D., & Balter, M.B. *Marijuana Use among Urban Adults.* Science *166,* 1544, 1969.

16 McGlothlin, W., Jamison, K., & Rosenblatt, S. *Marijuana and the Use of Other Drugs.* Nature *228,* 1227, 1970.

17 Murphy, H.B.M. *The Cannabis Habit. A Review of Recent Psychiatric Literature.* Bulletin on Narcotics *15,* 15, 1963.

18 Nyswander, M. *The Drug Addict as a Patient.* New York, 1956. Grune & Stratton.

19 Plaut, T.F.A. *Alcohol Problems. Report to the Nation by the Cooperative Commission on the Study of Alcoholism.* New York, 1967. Oxford University Press.

20 Popham, R.E. *The Jellinek Alcoholism Estimation Formula and its Application to Canadian Data.* Quarterly Journal of Studies on Alcohol *17,* 559, 1956.

21 Popham, R.E. *A.R.F. Research on Drugs Other Than Alcohol.* Toronto, 1970. Addiction Research Foundation.

22 Popham, R.E., Schmidt, W., & de Lint, J. *Epidemiologic Research Bearing on Legislative Attempts to Control Alcohol Consumption and Alcohol Problems.* Proceedings of a Symposium on Law and Drinking Behavior Held at Chapel Hill, N.C. 1970 (In press).

23 Roland, J.L., & Teste, M. *Le Cannabisme au Maroc.* Maroc Médical *37,* 694, 1958.

24 Schmidt, W., & de Lint, J. *Causes of Death of Alcoholics.* Quarterly Journal of Studies on Alcohol (In press).

25 Smart, R.G., Fejer, D., & White, J. *The Extent of Drug Use in Metropolitan Toronto Schools: A Study of Changes from 1968 to 1970.* Toronto, 1970. Addiction Research Foundation.

26 Smart, R.G., Laforest, L., & Whitehead, P.C. *The Epidemiology of Drug Use in Three Canadian Cities.* Addiction Research Foundation Substudy 1 – 7 & La & Wh – 70.

27 Smart, R.G., Whitehead, P., & Laforest, L. *The Prevention of Drug Abuse by Young People: an Argument Based on the Distribution of Drug Use.* Bulletin on Narcotics (In press).

28 Whitehead, P.C., Smart, R.G., & Laforest, L. *Multiple Drug Use Among Marihuana Smokers in Eastern Canada.* Addiction Research Foundation Substudy 2 – Wh & 7 & La – 70.

REFERENCES CHAPTER 8

1 Commission of Inquiry into the Non-Medical Use of Drugs. *Interim Report.* Ottawa, 1970. Queen's Printer for Canada.

2 Cook, S.J. Personal communication.

3 Cook, S.J. *Variations in Response to Illegal Drug Use. A Comparative Study of Official Narcotic Drug Policies in Canada, Great Britain, and the United States from 1920 to 1970.* Addiction Research Foundation Substudy 1 – Co & 11 – 70.

4 Ginsburg, A. *The Great Marihuana Hoax.* The Atlantic *218,* No. 5, 104, 1966.

5 Goode, E. *The Marijuana Smokers.* New York & London, 1970. Basic Books.

6 Kaplan, J. *Marijuana – The New Prohibition.* New York & Cleveland, 1970. World.

7 Lindesmith, A.R. *Introduction.* In: *The Marihuana Papers.* Solomon, D. (ed.) New York, 1966. Bobbs-Merrill.

8 Murphy, E.F. *The Black Candle.* Toronto, 1922, Allen.

9 Report by the Advisory Committee on Drug Dependence. *Cannabis.* London, 1968. H.M.S.O.

10 *Report of the Indian Hemp Drugs Commission – 1893-1894.* Simla, 1894. Government Printing Office. Reprinted: Kaplan, J. (ed.) *Marijuana, Report of the Indian Hemp Drugs Commission. 1893-1894.* Silver Spring, Maryland, 1969. Thos. Jefferson.

11 Smart, R.G., Fejer, D., & White, J. *The Extent of Drug Use in Metropolitan Toronto Schools: A Study of Changes from 1968 to 1970.* Toronto, 1970. Addiction Research Foundation.

12 Whitaker, R. *Drugs and the Law. The Canadian Scene.* Toronto, 1969. Methuen Publications.

13 Whitehead, P.C., Smart, R.G., & Laforest, L. *Multiple Drug Use among Marihuana Smokers in Eastern Canada.* Addiction Research Foundation Substudy 2 – Wh & 7 & La – 70.

REFERENCES CHAPTER 9

1 Anonymous. *Drogas – La Fuga Maldita.* Ercilla (Santiago, Chile) No. 1843, 35, 1970.

2 Brill, H., & Hirose, T. *The Rise and Fall of a Methamphetamine Epidemic: Japan 1945-55.* Seminars in Psychiatry *1,* 179, 1969.

3 Chopra, G.S. Personal communication.

4 Dewey, L.H. *Hemp.* Yearbook of the United States Department of Agriculture, p. 283, 1913.

5 Kalant, O.J. *The Amphetamines. Toxicity and Addiction.* Toronto, 1966. University of Toronto Press.

Index